MW01534800

Advancing a

Successful Business

Managing Your Organization

Advancing a
Successful Business

Managing Your Organization

abc
Book Publishing

Published by
ABC Book Publishing

AbcBookPublishing.com

Printed in U.S.A.

Advancing a Successful Business

Managing Your Organization

© Copyright 2009 by Richard A. Brott

ISBN: 1-60185-025-5

ISBN (EAN): 978-1-60185-025-6

All scripture quotations, unless otherwise indicated, are taken from the Holy Bible, New International Version®. NIV®. Copyright © 1973, 1978, 1984 by International Bible Society. Used by permission of Zondervan Publishing House. All rights reserved.

Other Versions used are:

AMP- Amplified Bible.

Amer. Std.-American Standard Version, 1901.

KJV-King James Version. Authorized King James Version.

NASB-Scripture taken from the New American Standard Bible, ©1960, 1962, 1963, 1968, 1971, 1972, 1973, 1975, 1977 by The Lockman Foundation. Used by permission.

-Scripture taken from the New King James Version. Copyright © 1979, 1980, 1982 by Thomas Nelson, Inc. Publishers. Used by permission. All rights reserved.

TLB-Verses marked (TLB) are taken from The Living Bible © 1971. Used by permission of Tyndale House Publishers, Inc., Wheaton, IL 60189. All rights reserved.

Scripture taken from THE MESSAGE: The Bible in Contemporary Language © 2002 by Eugene H. Peterson. All rights reserved.

All rights reserved, including the right to reproduce this book, or any portions thereof, in any form. No part of this book may be reproduced or transmitted in any form or by any means, electronic or mechanical, magnetic, chemical, optical, manual, or otherwise, including photocopying, recording, or by any information storage or retrieval system without written permission from Richard A. Brott. All rights for publishing this book or portions thereof in other languages are contracted by the author.

This publication is designed to provide interesting reading material and general information with regard to the subject matter covered. It is printed, distributed and sold with the understanding that neither the publisher nor the author is engaged in rendering religious, family, legal, accounting, investing, financial or other professional advice. If any such advice is required, the services of a competent professional person should be sought.

Every effort has been made to supply complete and accurate information. However, neither the publisher nor the author assumes any responsibility for its use, nor for any infringements of patents or other rights of third parties that would result.

First Edition, January 1, 2009

Richard A. Brott

All Rights Reserved

About the Author

Rich Brott holds a Bachelor of Science degree in Business and Economics and a Master of Business Administration.

Rich has served in an executive position of some very successful businesses. He has functioned on the board of directors for churches, businesses, and charities and served on a college advisory board. Rich has traveled to more than 25 countries on teaching assignments and business concerns.

Rich Brott has authored over thirty-five books including:

- *5 Simple Keys to Financial Freedom*
- *10 Life-Changing Attitudes That Will Make You a Financial Success*
- *15 Biblical Responsibilities Leading to Financial Wisdom*
- *30 Biblical Principles for Managing Your Money*
- *35 Keys to Financial Independence*
- *A Biblical Perspective on Giving Generously*
- *A Biblical Perspective on Tithing & Giving*
- *A Biblical Perspective on Tithing Faithfully*
- *Achieving Financial Alignment*
- *Activating Your Personal Faith to Receive*
- *Advancing a Successful Business*
- *All the Financial Scriptures in the Bible*
- *Basic Principles for Maximizing Your Personal Cash Flow*
- *Basic Principles of Conservative Investing*
- *Biblical Principles for Achieving Personal Success*
- *Biblical Principles for Becoming Debt Free*
- *Biblical Principles for Building a Successful Business*

- *Biblical Principles for Financial Success - Student Workbook*
- *Biblical Principles for Financial Success - Teacher Workbook*
- *Biblical Principles for Personal Evangelism*
- *Biblical Principles for Releasing Financial Provision*
- *Biblical Principles for Staying Out of Debt*
- *Biblical Principles for Success in Personal Finance*
- *Biblical Principles That Create Success Through Productivity*
- *Business, Occupations, Professions & Vocations In the Bible*
- *Developing a Successful Personal and Business Vision*
- *Establishing a Successful Business*
- *Family Finance Handbook*
- *Family Finance Student Workbook*
- *Family Finance Teacher Workbook*
- *How to Receive Prosperity and Provision*
- *Maximizing Your Business Success*
- *Prosperity Has a Purpose*
- *Public Relations for the Local Church*
- *Successful Time Management*

He and his wife Karen, have been married for 37 years. Rich Brott resides in Portland, Oregon, with his wife, three children, son-in-law and granddaughter.

Dedication

I dedicate this book to all of you promising young entrepreneurs who have yet to become businessmen and businesswomen, but have already begun to develop seeds of greatness within you.

Your chances of success and accomplishment will increase as you begin to serve and receive input from mentors whose paths you will cross. You are destined for greatness as you take advantage of the many wonderful learning opportunities you will encounter.

Table of Contents

Advancing a Successful Business
Managing Your Organization

Introduction

Business focus is an integral part of your ability to advance and build your business into something beyond mediocrity. Staying focused on your vision and purpose is very key.

Nothing significant is ever achieved without focus. If it's worth getting, it must be the focus of your attention at all times. Focus begins with a sense of purpose, mission and vision. This is your sense of direction, your road map, your life track for the business. It's where you are headed.

Business goals support this vision. When your vision is clear, your goals are clear. When your goals are clear, you will become more focused. When you have a sense of business purpose; when you have determined your goals for each area of your business, then you need a series of action plans to pursue them. This becomes your business strategy and tactic for advancement and achievement. This strategy is what you plan to do and how you plan to do it.

But having a sense of why you are in business and what your business mission and purpose is not enough. Habits of good business practices must be part of your business D.N.A. A business must also have good management practices if it is to become successful and remain that way. The importance of keeping projects on schedule as well as action plans on task, is a daily responsibility. These tasks must have weekly oversight or your regular routine will become a crisis.

Crisis management is management by reaction. Some people manage by crisis. The *"let it happen to you"* way. They react somewhat like putting out a forest fire...working harder, but not smarter. On the other hand, planned management is the anticipation in advance of possible future events. It is the *"make it happen...preventive maintenance"* ...the way you want things to happen style.

Your ability to form a group of competent achievers that can solve business problems, make critical decisions and communicate in every area of business is essential to being successful. This requires the building of effective teams.

Certainly there are course corrections to every strategy, and making those necessary changes as well as removing obstacles and roadblocks to growth require effective and efficient implementation.

A growing company does not continue without great business productivity, timely follow-through and effective leadership. Advancing a Successful Business is not automatic and will not happen without a steady hand at the helm backed by a great team who stays alert and motivated.

I hope you will benefit from the insights gleaned within these pages.

Rich Brott

Chapter 1

Habits of Success

It may seem odd to begin a business book by talking about habits of success. But over the years, I have found that habits, whether good or bad, positive or destructive, that are formed and practiced by individuals are carried from the their personal life into their work environments. Whether you are the owner, a stockholder, a business partner, a manager or a staff person, forming good productive habits will advance both you and your business along in positive, efficient and productive ways.

Business success can be made or broken by the habits you form. Our habits have great influence upon our success in life. Habits can be major obstacles to becoming successful. Habits can be the foundation of your successes. Most everything you do is the result of habits. All habits are learned…and that is good news!

We first form habits; then habits form us!

We first form habits; then habits form us! On our road to success, if we do not consciously form good habits, we will unconsciously form bad ones. So we form habits both unconsciously or consciously. Habits are not instincts; they are acquired reactions. They don't "just happen," they are caused. What we continue to do over and over again becomes a habit. Our lives become the sum total of our habits. Once you have determined the original cause of a habit, it is within your power either to accept or to reject it.

Every person who is successful has simply formed the habits of doing things that failures dislike doing and will not do. It is just as easy to form the habit of succeeding as it is to succumb to the habit of failure. The harvest we reap in our lives is measured by the attitudes and habits we cultivate. Our habits can be the basis for success or the basic for failure. As such they can predict the future. What you are doing now is what will determine your future.

Our lives become the sum total of our habits.

Your behavior is based on the accumulation of all your experiences. Most of your actions and reactions are automatic, unconscious responses to the habits you have formulated over the years. Bad habits can become major roadblocks to your success. Between the "where you are today" and the "where you want to be tomorrow" often stands the "habits you are bound by today."

Your habits keep you "running in place." In the absence of some outside influence, or a personal decision on your part to do something different, your habits will keep you doing, reacting, and being the same as you've always been.

When habits become major obstacles to your happiness or performance, they must be discarded completed or modified to bring them into line with your life. Bad habits include being late for appointments or late in completing assignments. Successful people are always punctual and dependable. Successful people respect the time of others and keep their commitments.

Proverbs 23:7 had this to say about our habits of thought. "For as he thinks in his heart, so is he". (NKJV) Bad thought patterns and habits can be very detrimental to your success. Whatever you think about continually, you will create in your life. Negative, self-limiting thoughts hurt you more than almost anything else. You live in a mental world. Nothing physical around you has much meaning except the meaning you give it with your thoughts. If you can change your way of thinking, you can change your results.

> *Between the "where you are today" and the "where you*
> *want to be tomorrow" often stands the "habits you are*
> *bound by today."*

Habits are only good as long as they serve your purpose. Good habits should continually enrich and improve your life. A good life is the result of automatic ways you respond and react to what's going on around you. Habits that are no longer consistent with your life purposes must be changed.

Changing bad habits is essential to the quality of your life. Unless you have already reached some level of excellence or perfection, you are "right now", "today," living with one or more (maybe one hundred or more) habits that should be discarded. Bad habits are easy to form. Many just form automatically by default. Bad habits are hard to live with.

Good habits are hard to form. They never form automatically. Good habits are easy to live with. Your #1 priority should be to form good, purpose-fulfilling, goal-reaching habits. Don't be controlled by bad habits. Make good habits your master.

A very insightful proverb whose author is unknown, follows.

> *Plant a thought, harvest an act.*
> *Plant an act, harvest a habit.*
> *Plant a habit, harvest a character.*
> *Plant a character, harvest a destiny.*

What about your regular habits. Do they lead to the blessing of God? Can God supernaturally provide for you based on your habitual acts? Are they principled, ethical and biblically based?

Habits are often the basis for business success or business failure. Although people form many habits, both good and bad, habits are the basis for the future. You can form habits unconsciously or consciously. On our road to business success, if we do not consciously form good habits, we will unconsciously form bad ones. Habits are not instincts; they are acquired reactions. They don't "just happen", they are caused. Once you have determined the original cause of a habit, it is within your power either to accept or to reject it.

It's not what happens to you that counts as much as how you react to what happens.

Every person who is successful has simply formed the habits of doing things that God can bless. Success and failure, happiness and unhappiness are largely the result of habit. It is just as easy to form the habit of succeeding as it is to surrender to the habit of failure.

The attitudes and habits we cultivate, measure the harvest we reap in our lives. Successful people can be found everywhere. Successful businesspersons are everywhere. They are not extraordinary people, although many have lived extraordinary lives. All have particular qualities in common. These are not qualities you inherit, rather you must develop them through education and through hard work.

It's not what happens to you that counts as much as how you react to what happens. All successful people pattern their personal and work lives after biblical principles, are productive and efficient in business and actively seek the wisdom of God.

Here are some things to watch as you build your business.

Accept Responsibility

Attitude – Great business persons share one characteristic. They take obstacles and failure and convert them into motivators.

Be Flexible To Obstacles

Be Persistent

Break Your Habits - Ask yourself, "Is there another way to accomplish this?"

Breakdown Barriers To Creativity - Find the barriers to developing and implementing new ideas and remove them. Old barriers such as, "It won't work any other way; it's against policy; people won't embrace it; it's against operating procedures" just don't fit in today's management culture.

Change As Necessary

Compassion - To offer compassion is always one of life's rich experiences.

Concentrate On Your Priorities

Confidentiality - Don't share information you know to be confidential or that you have been asked to keep to yourself.

Determination - Be persistent, especially when you fail.

Develop a learning process - Failure isn't failure as long as we learn from it.

Effort - The only way to get something you want is to put in the effort required to get it. There are no easy answers, no get-rich-quick schemes, just plenty of scams which will only serve to derail you from your potential success.

Embrace New Perspectives - Forget your traditional perspective and approach change from other viewpoints.

Exercise - Vigorous activity strengthens your body and helps to relieve stress. Medical experts insist that people who exercise regularly, age more slowly, remain healthier and feel better than those who do not.

Giving back to others - The most treasured aspect of being successful is that it enables you to help others achieve the same.

Honesty - Always speak and live the truth.

Mentors - Learn to ask for help and support, and find resources for getting the help you need.

Minimize Interruptions That Take Away Your Focus

Passionate pursuit – Seek the favor of God with passion.

Patience - Whether you're eager to speak next or to reach your next goal, accept that "your turn will come." This doesn't mean settling for inaction, however. Being patient isn't the same as being complacent.

Peace - Excesses of any kind can be hazardous to your physical and mental health. One must experience peace in body, soul and spirit. Take care of your body, but do not forget to care for your soul and spirit. Your emotional and spiritual health are just as necessary as your physical health.

Persistence - This is perhaps the most essential quality needed to attain success both in your professional career and in your personal life. If you throw in the towel every time you face adversity, you'll never know how a winner feels. When the going gets rough, stay in the ring and slug it out.

Practice Creativity - Try new ideas, new solutions to problems, new ways of doing things, etc.

Punctuality - Be on time, every time, every meeting, every deadline, every part of your life.

Purity - Reject anything that lowers your personal standards or the standards of those you serve.

Responsibility - Be trustworthy and dependable.

Rest - Exhaustion and stress are a dangerous combination. Do not let yourself bear the high stress of building personal dreams while at the same time depriving your body the necessary rest and relaxation that it desperately needs. By getting "rest" during the night, you'll be your "best" during the daytime.

Review Your Progress

Seek Help

Self-control - Make wise decisions. Don't let emotion lead you astray or let a fear of being wrong hold you back from making decisions.

Setting goals – Successful business people turn passion into practical reality.

Think In Positives And Potential - Negative thinking inhibits growth and potential.

Thoughtfulness - Think of others before yourself.

Try Out New Ways And Ideas - Don't accept, "It won't work any other way" until you've tried alternative solutions.

View Failures As Opportunities - One of the most common aspects of success is the ability -- and the willingness -- to accept the challenges failure presents.

Vision - Without a vision, without purpose, no goals can be met. A lack of goals leads to a lack of planning and inaction. Know what your purpose in this life is all about.

Set a vision before you. Fill your mind with an image of what can be and what you will accomplish. Let everything in your life revolve around your vision and you'll take on track in spite of varied circumstances. Vision gives focus. Have a vision!

Chapter 2

Managing Your Business

Management Styles

Every successful business has disciplined managers. These people know the discipline required to run a business. As a business owner or manager, everything you do, every decision you make, has some effect on the bottom line. Always think of the bottom line before you make a decision. The importance of keeping projects on schedule, action plans on task, is a weekly responsibility. These tasks must have weekly oversight or your schedule will become a crisis.

Be clear with others about the need to maintain a manufacturing or sales schedule. Sharing relevant information with employees, partners and investors is also very important. A seasoned manager knows that a bad attitude or poor customer service person, translates into poor sales and the lack of repeat business. The person who knows how has a job; the disciplined and seasoned business manager who knows why is the boss.

Everything you do, every decision you make, has some effect on the bottom line.

A six word formula for real business success is this.

Think things through, then follow through.

There are two kinds of management styles. They are management by *crisis* and *planned management*. You could also call them *reactive* and *proactive* management.

Crisis Management:

Crisis management is management by reaction. Some people manage by crisis. The "let it happen to you" way. They react somewhat like putting out a forest fire...working harder, but not smarter.

Planned Management:

Planned management is the anticipation in advance of possible future events. It is the "make it happen...preventive maintenance" (the way you want things to happen) style. No surprises! Management by working smarter. Rather than always reacting to events and current circumstances that continually change, proactive planning analyzes business environmental forces and makes course corrections that places the business where it needs to be next month, next year and throughout the next decade.

Planned management problem prevention is an important process. When a company has passed the point of "putting out fires" and have started looking ahead for ways to prevent them, it will have achieved a major milestone.

Proactive planning analyzes business environmental forces and makes the necessary course corrections.

How does planned management happen and how do you communicate this style to and through your staff? You must be sure your business staff is on board with preventive maintenance. This means making sure there are no surprises. Some ways for you to have a style of management that could be described as *"planned management"* follow.

Act now. Fix it, move it, try it, explore it, and go for it. You probably will not fail for lack of good ideas, but you will always fail if we do not act on them. So be opportunistic and take risks. Set deadlines, and if you miss them, set new ones. Above all, act!

Be a leader. Be someone who sets an example for others to follow.

Be a successful manager who is a good leader.

Be a mobile communicator. Walk around, talk, look, listen, and spread the word. Communication also means listening, so let your employees know that you want to hear from them, and then hear them out. The key to communication is attitude. Be willing to become a partner in a joint process, not a commander in the field. Partnership is not absolute authority, but rather a productivity tool. Time after time, it is the frontline person who knows the solution to the problem.

Be enthusiastic. A happy environment is a productive environment, so play the company cheerleader and emphasize a can-do approach to work. Enthusiasm is contagious but so is defeatism.

Be flexible and persistent in the pursuit of defined goals. Let your employed professionals know what your objectives are both short and long term. Nothing is more important than mobilizing everyone toward a common goal.

Create a trusting environment that encourages learning.

Encourage innovation.

Encourage others to express their ideas.

Expect and accept only quality. To achieve quality, you must ask for it, expect it, require it, and reward it. Excellence breeds excellence. Without quality, you will not have any customers, and without customers, you will not have a business.

Express a viewpoint from your perspective, but be open to what others think.

First things first, every day. Get organized and disciplined.

Focus on excellence, not perfection.

Focus on team building. Address issues that build barriers to effective group communication.

Involve others in developing "common functional visions".

Know where you are going and how you plan to get there.

Measure everyone's productivity - including your own. Unless you are measuring your productivity, you will not know whether you are on course, off course, or ready to crash. Measures can and should be simple. The best are usually the ones developed by the individuals or groups being measured.

Persistence rules. Presented with problems, you, the successful entrepreneur, must attack them head on. Quitting cannot be in your vocabulary. Giving up must be a foreign language. Negativism is unnatural. The measure of an individual's success is not what he or she achieves, rather what he/she is able to overcome. Many different people have been credited with the same statement. It is this. "If you always do what you've done, you'll always get what you've gotten." So if you want something different, and you don't like what you're getting, do something different!

Seek out and remove obstacles to productivity. Let employees know that you are serious about eliminating productivity barriers by organizing a "search and destroy" mission. Ask all of your people to list what they see as obstacles to their own productivity, then have them list the obstacles they see to the company's overall productivity and efficiency. When the obstacles are clearly identified, have the courage to remove them no matter whose territory is invaded.

Set clear objectives and milestones to check your progress toward your goals.

To be a successful competitor, you have to be a successful manager.

Understand the importance of great follow-through. Follow-through is vital to the success of all businesses. No goals are every reached without great follow-through. To do so takes great discipline. Personal discipline is a key to success. Another key to success is persistence. Persistence in maintaining a firm grasp on every part of your business plan. This means keeping at the important things and never let them slide. Yet another vital key to success is personal business accountability. You are accountable to your business plan. The plan makes you accountable to your banker, investors, clients and board of directors. You will always be accountable to someone.

Use your imagination. People who are not successful think within the box; no creative thinking, no new ideas, no new possibilities, etc. There are always options; new ways to approach a problem, new ideas to imagine, new ways of doing things. Successful people are truly creative. They envision alternatives. They are curious, always trying out new possibilities. The entrepreneur achieves success through innovation.

Nothing is more important than mobilizing everyone toward a common goal.

Measuring Your Progress

All businesses require measurements of activity or progress. List some of the milestones to be reached under each category so that you can measure your improvement from pre-determined points of progress.

✓   Minimal

        (Some Progress)

        A. _____

        B. _____

        C. _____

✓   Acceptable

        (Consistent Movement)

        A. _____

        B. _____

        C. _____

✓   Outstanding

        (Ahead of the Game)

        A. _____

        B. _____

        C. _____

Conducting Productive Meetings

Meetings are a fact of life in today's business world. Yet many people feel that they last too long, occur too often, and don't solve enough problems.

"The most productive meetings last under an hour," says Jack McAlinden, head of a New York-based communications consulting firm. Despite this, the average meeting lasts about two hours, according to a survey by the 3M Meeting Management Institute in Minnesota.

The cure to excessive meeting length is better organization. You can become better organized by paying attention to the basics of meeting management.

1. Handle the issues another way.

If the purpose of the meeting is to make an announcement, put out a memo instead. Make a phone call to deal with status reports instead of having a meeting. Let project leaders hand in written reports instead of having a weekly conference.

2. Use timing as a tool to make meetings more efficient.

Many successful businesses hold their sales meetings early in the morning, before the typical business open its doors. Or hold the meeting at 11:30 a.m. or 4:30 p.m. so people won't want to extend it beyond what is necessary.

3. Invite only those who really need to be there.

Limit each department to one representative. Resist inviting people for purely personal or political reasons.

4. Prepare a specific agenda and publish it in advance.

This gives everyone a chance to prepare. After the meeting, issue follow-up notes to make it clear what each person is assigned to do.

5. Keep people on the subject.

If discussion strays from the agenda, ask the person to see you after the meeting to discuss the issue.

If you master these guidelines, chances are your meetings will run smoothly and accomplish their purpose. Your staff may even start looking forward to meetings!

Becoming More Valuable

Here is some advise that you can give to your employed professionals.

1.   When listening, concentrate!

Many of us listen and hear only about 50% of what is being said. You can avoid mistakes and backtracking and establish a reputation of only having to be told once if you listen with full concentration.

2.   Become solution oriented!

Make a habit of spotting ways to cut costs, eliminate inefficiency, etc. in each project that you are involved. Research your potential solutions thoroughly before moving ahead.

3.   Be aware of your shortcomings!

Do you lack when it comes to communication skills? Do you lack needed industry skills? Do you have deficiencies in specific areas of your business responsibilities? Do something about your shortcomings. First be honest with yourself and recognize you need to improve. Then get a plan together to do just that.

4.   *Continue the learning process!*

Place yourself on a rigid on-going educational process. Develop general knowledge as well as specialized knowledge. Develop job-related skills.

5.   Learn related jobs.

Know how to do the jobs of those around you. You will become more valuable to your business.

Chapter 3

Solving Business Problems

Every business difficulty requires some action to correct the challenge, obstacle or problem. The challenge is to determine the proper course of action. Usually the best way to begin that choice is to gather all of the facts and begin to ask a number of relevant questions.

In their article on selecting a consultant, Kirchhoff and Rinehart suggest that the first step in solving business problems is to "collect and analyze the facts, making sure to separate important and relevant information from superficial and irrelevant data.

- ✓ Clearly State The Problem
- ✓ Determine Gain Or Loss In Solving The Problem
- ✓ Identify Alternative Methods & Solutions
- ✓ State Cost/Benefit Of Each Alternative
- ✓ Delegate Action Steps
- ✓ Begin Implementation
- ✓ Evaluate Progress

Problem solving can be benefited by asking the following questions.

- • What would you like to become clear today?
- • What is it that is unclear?
- • What would you like to achieve?

- What solutions have been attempted so far?
- What is your attitude regarding the situation?
- What benefits do you receive from having this situation?
- What is the reality of the problem?
- What would you like to see happen?
- What else would you like to see happen?
- What do you need to do at this time?
- How would your business be different if this situation were to change?
- What one thing are you willing to change to make this be what you would like it to be?

Furthermore, once you have determined possible solutions, you will need to choose between available alternatives. To help you think clearly through this process and eventually to be able to decide which solution is appropriate, ask yourself these questions.

- Does This Alternative Align With My Purpose, Mission, & Vision?
- Will This Alternative Help Me Reach My Pre-Determined Goal?
- Does This Solution Violate Principle Or Biblical Truth?
- Does This Solution Meet My Long Term Needs Or Is It A Temporary Fix?
- Do Those Around Me Buy Into This Alternative?
- Will This Solution Create Additional Problems?
- Why Should This Alternative Be Selected Over Others?

Be answering these simple questions, you should be able to see the alternative that best fits your answers.

Questions of Efficiency

Some business problems originate through lack of business efficiency. Is your business organization operating in its greatest possible efficiency? Here are some questions to help you objectively answer that question.

- Do you clearly define all functions within the business organization?

- Does each employed professional know to whom he or she is responsible to?

- Have you made sure that each person only has one supervisor?

- Have you eliminated all duplicate functions and areas of overlap?

- Does any supervisor or facilitator have too few or too many people reporting to him or her?

- Does your business organizational system allow delegation to the lowest possible level?

- Do you encourage the free exchange of ideas and flow of information across functional lines?

Chapter 4

Instituting Effective Leadership

Business Leadership Skills

The subject of leadership and the skills required to be an effective leader seems endless. In their book, *"Organizational Communication,"* Eisenberg and Goodall note that *"leadership is perhaps the most studied phenomenon in organizational behavior."* "Leadership - A Communication Perspective," by Hackman & Johnson, states that some primary approaches for understanding leadership have evolved over the past ninety years. One approach to understanding leadership is the "Situational Approach." It is based on the idea that "traits, skills, and behaviors necessary for effective leadership vary from situation to situation."

This approach depends greatly on one's *"interpersonal skills,"* which vary from person to person. Not only do circumstances change, but people vary in traits and personalities, and it's a fact that business environments are continuously changing. The communicator's interpersonal skills help him/her to be an effective leader.

Listed below are six interpersonal skills listed by Hackman & Johnson which are necessary and important for practical and meaningful leadership.

Six interpersonal skills for leadership communication:

- Creativity in Dealing with People
- Evaluation of Employees
- Tension Relieving in Stressful Situations
- Negotiating and Compromising
- Flexibility with People
- Encouragement of Co-workers

Creativity in Dealing with People

Creativity is the ability to solve people problems in a novel, yet appropriate fashion. Sometimes creativity means finding alternative solutions to old problems. Other times, it means recognizing that a difficult situation can be solved by the implementation of new approaches. Creativity is applied to both decisions about work related tasks and decisions about people. The creative leader will try out new ways of dealing with employees. If one technique does not work with a particular person, the creative leader tries another one.

The effective business manager and leader must be able to focus on the nature of the job rather than on personalities of the employees. The manager should project a strong commitment to getting the job done right. At the same time, he or she must try to convince the employees of the job's importance to them personally. This skill enables the leader to play down personality conflicts and encourage the group to focus on the task.

Evaluation of Employees

It is part of a business manager's duties to evaluate employees by talking with them about their job performance. Some leaders find it easy to pay a compliment but difficult to offer criticism, even if the criticism is constructive. Everyone wants to be liked. Offering criticism and encouraging subordinates to accept constructive evaluation is part of the leadership task. Evaluation takes more than comments such as, "Good job," or "It looks OK," or "You could have done better." These comments are much too general. Specific comments that compare the work of the person being evaluated to an established standard make for a good evaluation. In order to properly utilize "evaluation" as an interpersonal skill necessary for meaningful leadership, the following things must be known.

To be an effective evaluator, the leader must understand the task. The task includes what a person is supposed to be doing and what the performance expectations are. Normally the evaluation will require the leader to compare the employee's level of skill with an established criterion for success.

In defining the task, leaders must communicate frequently and clearly. They must ask the questions:

1. *"Are my directions and instructions easy to understand?"*
2. *"Have I communicated my vision clearly?"*
3. *"Do I avoid snags by explaining matters carefully in advance?"*
4. *"Do my employees know what they are doing?*
5. *"Do my employees know why they are doing things?*

The effective leader must consider the following things when evaluating the employee's attitude. People differ widely in their ability to accept criticism. If heavy criticism is going to induce a moderately successful worker to withdraw, it will be more purposeful and meaningful if it is lightened just a bit and carefully worded.

An employee's attitudes and values heavily influence their job performance. If the ultimate goal is to improve the performance of the employee, then a personalized and individualized approach must be designed for each person. A good evaluator can perceive the attitudes of employees fairly and accurately and can choose the best strategy in each case.

Leaders must remember the following points when considering an employee's potential. It is important to remember that the primary reason for doing individual evaluations is to improve job performance. Not all workers are equally productive.

Leaders need to develop skills that will enable them to determine which employees are working up to potential and which are not. By knowing an employee's background, education and work experience, a manager can understand his or her strengths and weaknesses. This enables the leader to evaluate progress as the need arises.

Tension Relieving in Stressful Situations

Conflict and tension are the by-products of just about any work situation. A good manager will not be surprised when two or three employees engage in petty bickering or heated exchanges. This is human nature. The leader can use certain techniques to bring the work group back together. A joke intended to poke a little harmless fun at one's self or at the group sometimes reduces tension -- especially if it is related to the group's current task. Of course, humor must be in good taste and never at someone else's expense. Humor is a tension reliever, but careless laughter can get out of control and reduce productivity.

Role reversal occurs when the leader asks each side to state the other side's position. The situation can be taken one step further by having each side write down the other side's position, and then suggest how the conflict might be resolved. This helps to see all sides of the issue and presents a more complete picture of the problem to be solved.

Creative brainstorming resembles role reversal. Conflicting parties are encouraged to work together for the purpose of generating a wide range of possible solutions to the conflict. Idea generation, no matter how insignificant some may seem, has proven to be very beneficial to this company. The brainstorming process seems to create an atmosphere of cooperation among opposing viewpoints, while at the same time relieving tensions that may have been building.

Negotiating and Compromising

Good managers should be able to negotiate, not only with their employees, but also with their peers and with their own superiors. The ability to help work out compromises is an important tool in decision making. The ability to cooperate and compromise goes hand-in-hand with the ability to bring out the best in people.

A good leader must know how to negotiate with those above, beside, and below. No structured formula can fit every situation. Negotiating skills enable the leader to develop a program, plan or idea that will work. Compromising may mean working out an agreement between employees who disagree. It may mean trying to reach a settlement with the organization when the work group's objectives have not been fully met. It may simply mean reconciling people who file official protests and grievances with those they are protesting against.

Compromise and negotiation consists of accepting or rejecting an offer after one has calculated the potential costs. It therefore requires skill in calculating costs and expertise in proposing attractive alternatives.

Flexibility with People

Flexibility is the ability to face each problem without a highly structured, rigid set of expectations. Each problem is both similar to and different from previous problems. Routine and innovative leadership will both be required to solve it. The typical organization changes daily as its environments change. The condition of the outside world changes. The nature of each task and the people who do it change.

The leader who approaches each problem with a fixed set of ideas about how to solve it may find that those ideas don't work anymore. Flexibility in leadership will enable a person to generate options -- that is to create a range of alternative solutions to each problem.

Encouragement of Co-workers

Encouragement is the ability to inspire the work group to produce. It is also the ability to develop participation. A climate that makes members want to participate is essential to effective group problem solving. Business owners, managers and leaders must show faith in their employees.

It is important to organize and delegate, but then step aside. Employees should be encouraged to speak up and contribute to ongoing discussions. A good leader will welcome suggestions and prompt subordinates to think creatively.

Every leader should offer praise for even the smallest accomplishments. This makes employees feel good about themselves and gives them the confidence and encouragement they need to carry on. Leaders must use every opportunity to point out progress.

Giving employees credit for any praise that comes to the company from outside customers is extremely profitable. By noticing the little victories and not just the foul-ups, leaders quickly gain respect, loyalty, and commitment from those around them.

The leader must keep the lines of communication open with the group. The arbitrary closing of a channel may preclude the participation and contribution essential to an effective work group. Managers who stifle ideas and close communication channels are practicing poor leadership.

Effective Leadership Skills

Leadership and management are very different from each other. Leadership has to do with direction while management with organizing and mobilizing an organization to go in that direction.

Leadership says:

- I have a vision.
- Here is where we're going.
- Look…there is your destiny.

Management says:

- Here is how we will get there.
- Let's get started.
- Here is your roadmap.

Leadership has to do with direction while management with organizing and mobilizing an organization to go in that direction.

Below are some effective leadership and decision-making skills.

- ✦ Benevolent
- ✦ Charismatic
- ✦ Communicator
- ✦ Delegator
- ✦ Discerner
- ✦ Enthusiastic
- ✦ Ethical
- ✦ Inspirational

✦ Intellectually Stimulating

✦ Interest In Growth of Subordinates

✦ Interpersonal Skills

✦ Listener

✦ Motivator

✦ Organizer

✦ Role Model

✦ Transformational Person

✦ Visionary

A basic function of a good leader is to inspire people to their best efforts. The person who concentrates only on details, on cost figures or on technical matters may become an expert, but not a leader. Experts know what should be done; leaders know what should be done and how to get people to do it.

Most people recognize good leadership when they see it, but what is it that makes a good leader? More importantly, how can you develop the qualities that will make you a good leader? Stogdill says that, "a person does not become a leader by virtue of the possession of some combination of traits, but the pattern of personal characteristics of the leader must bear some relevant relationship to the characteristics, activities, and goals of the followers."

You can improve your leadership ability only if you understand the personal tools available to you; your limitations and potentialities. Don't try to force yourself into a role that makes you feel awkward and uncomfortable. Remember that there's no "right" or "wrong" way to be a leader. This does not mean that leadership skills cannot be learned. Your success as a business leader calls for the blending of your personal capacities with sound leadership principles, continually applied.

Leadership is not bossiness, nor is it stubbornness. It's not blind insistence on having your own way. The effective leaders, the ones you want to follow, never force a response. Instead, they challenge you with the privilege of performing for them. Leaders visualize what they want to accomplish and how they want to do it.

Leaders acknowledge viewpoints other than their own. They let others inform them while holding on to fundamental beliefs and principles. When listening to others they acknowledge the validity of their beliefs. By doing so, leaders take the first step that will allow people to follow them, whether they agree wholeheartedly or not. It's easier for people to follow your way of thinking when you acknowledge theirs.

Leaders know how to motivate.

Leaders know how to motivate. Good leaders communicate their enthusiasm for a project and infect their groups with the same urgency and dedication they feel. They build a fire, and stroke it with praise, constructive criticism, and support for the group effort. Leaders are coaches who'll get their hands dirty when necessary.

Business leaders are visionaries, but they are realistic. They understand what they're asking of their groups and how their goals will impact the group. They understand everyone's function within the group. They set their sights high, but not so high that the goal is out of reach. At the same time leaders are learners. They learn from their successes and failures. They learn from the people around them. Leaders nurture their ability to see the big picture without losing critical details.

Leaders are also confident. Through learning and experience, leaders develop self-confidence, and distill a consistent set of values from the world around them. Oliver Wendell Holmes once attended a meeting at which he was the shortest man present. "Doctor Holmes," a friend chuckled, "I should think you'd feel rather small among us big fellows." "I do," answered Holmes. "I feel like a dime among a lot of pennies." Holmes had discovered the secret of accepting himself for what he was... and then exploiting it.

Leaders shape self-confidence, experience, and values into a personal integrity that commands respect and fosters trust. People who are in positions of leadership are able to inspire. Leaders are not necessarily brilliant strategists or the most able administrators. They may even lack technical expertise. But leaders do one thing well; they know how to inspire others and motivate them for the task at hand.

A good leader doesn't shy away from responsibility or hard work. He/she doesn't quit when faced with unexpected obstacles. The mental fuel that motivates him/her is a continuing eagerness to grow and improve in all levels. But a successful leader is also realistic about his/her goals. He/she doesn't waste time reaching for the moon.

Self-confidence is an indispensable asset to a good leader, because it is communicated to others. People respect the person who genuinely knows what he/she is doing. When one develops leadership experience, he/she can base real confidence on fact rather than fiction.

The ability to cooperate goes hand in hand with the ability to bring out the best in people. A good leader must know how to cooperate with those above, beside, and below. No pat formula can fit every situation. There are ways to be cooperative and stimulate cooperation in others.

It is important for every leader to show respect for each employed associate. Superiors and subordinates are equally entitled to respect. Showing the same consideration that you would like to receive pays dividends. Leaders cannot fake interest; insincerity is easy to spot. Leaders should be taught to show faith in their subordinates. It is important to organize and delegate, but then step aside.

Every business leader makes decisions. Sometimes they turn out right and sometimes they turn out wrong. Either way, the decisions are made. Leadership decisions are often required to be made quickly. Does this mean that we're doomed to failure if we are not the type who can jump to rapid conclusions? Not at all.

Good decisions are seldom arrived at haphazardly. They are based on sound problem-solving techniques. I use the following guidelines when I need to make a tough decision.

- Understanding what I am actually expected to decide is a necessity.

- Getting as much background information about the problem as possible is a personal requirement.

- Calling on the resources of my associates is mandatory; especially those with specialized training in the area involved.

- It is important for me to check my thinking to make sure that my own attitude is free from personal bias and irrelevant emotional factors.

- Listing all possible alternatives and analyzing them carefully is vital. I then list the probable consequences of each potential action.

- If I am able to compare the problem to previous circumstances, I do so to provide helpful precedents. Reviewing the results of past decisions often sheds light on present circumstances.

- Once I have made a decision, it is announced as soon as possible and I'm not afraid to back it up.

Managers are people who do things right and leaders are people who do the right thing.

Leadership vs. Management

Leadership is not the same as management, although it may at times include some management responsibilities. Warren Bennis notes that "managers are people who do things right and leaders are people who do the right thing." I have found the following guidelines helpful in working with people.

- Show respect for your subordinates. They'll return it.
- Treat everyone equally and fairly.
- Concentrate on removing the cause of the error.
- Show regard for the feelings of others.
- Do your reprimanding in private.
- Think your instructions out beforehand so that they are communicated clearly.
- Pass along compliments to those you work with.
- Be big enough to admit your mistakes.

These are some things a leader should never do.

- Use your position of authority to badger others.
- Show partiality or favoritism.
- Bicker when something goes wrong.
- Scold a subordinate in front of his/her associates.
- Issue vague or garbled instructions.
- Hoard credit - or compliments - when they come your way.
- Try to shift the blame on others when something goes wrong.
- Complain about your subordinates or "run them down." Their errors are a direct reflection upon you.

As a business leader, always be sure that you have made your expectations clear. Use a clear concise written position description to spell out organizational policies and job duties. After explaining these expectations, have the employee/volunteer sign the agreement and keep a copy. The specifics of this contract can then be used as a benchmark for identifying problems and evaluating performance.

Communicate often. Leaders communicate frequently and clearly. They ask the question, "Are my directions and instructions easy to understand? Have I communicated my vision clearly? Do I avoid unnecessary snags by explaining matters carefully in advance? Do my subordinates know why they are doing things, in addition to what they are doing?"

Be liberal in praise. Every leader should use a lot of praise for even the smallest accomplishments. This will make followers feel good about themselves and give them the confidence they need to carry on. Leaders must use every opportunity to point out their progress and remind them of how far they've come in mastering a task. Passing along any praise that comes to the organization and giving followers/volunteers/employees the credit is profitable. By noticing the little victories and not just the foul-ups, leaders quickly gain respect, loyalty, and commitment from those around you.

Take an interest. Essential to successful leadership is the ability to take an interest in subordinates. Find out what works and what does not work for them. In an employment situation, find out if they are working at jobs best suited to their individual abilities? Does the leader know anything about them personally...what their problems are; what makes them tick?

Keep morale high. Encourage team spirit. Compliment a person when he/she deserves it. According to House and Mitchell, the ability to motivate followers is influenced by a leader's communication style. One of these styles is "Achievement-Oriented Leadership." This communication is "focusing on goal attainment and accomplishment, emphasizing the achievement of excellence by demonstrating confidence in the ability of follows to achieve their goals."

Are followers reaching for the proper goals? Is the company culture and climate one of rewarding excellence? Do subordinates have a feeling of belonging, of being needed on the job? Are they briefed on the overall picture?

Everyone needs a feeling of personal worth and the knowledge that he/she is appreciated. The ability to respond to this need and bring out the best in each individual and in each group is the mark of a good leader. Do followers desire to do their best? Are they given a sense of pride in their work? Do they receive support from those in leadership positions?

Leaders must have a vision. They must stress the big picture. Employees and volunteers often feel unimportant when they're at the bottom of the organization. Show them how their job fits in and explain why their efforts are important to the smooth functioning of the operation. Let them know how valuable their contribution is. Helping followers feel needed will foster cooperation and motivation.

Show appreciation publicly. A pat on the back is always nice, but there are times when good work deserves something extra. Use company/organizational meetings and other occasions to recognize individuals for their special contributions. Mention people by name and specifically describe the good job they did.

Leaders have the ability to make the task seem enjoyable and rewarding. A happy atmosphere will make even low-level jobs seem pleasant. Having a sense of humor can go a long way. Laughter is especially important in stressful situations. When an person causes a crisis, try to keep things light and wait until later to discuss the mistake.

Warren Bennis wrote an article entitled "On Becoming a Leader." In it he says this about leadership; "You are your own best teacher; Accept responsibility, blame no one; You can learn anything you want to learn; and true understanding comes from reflecting on your experience." Leaders are not born, they are developed. With the proper amount of training, experience, initiative and attitude, any person can become the leader they want to be while effecting a positive influence upon their environment.

Attributes of Focused Business Leaders

✓ Integrity

Focused business leaders honor their commitments and promises.

✓ Congruity

Business leaders walk their talk, practice what they preach.

✓ Reliability

Business leaders support their team members. They are present when expected.

✓ Constancy

The catchphrase of business leaders is "no surprises." Leaders generate expected results time after time; they stay the course.

Delegation

Let's talk about delegation and what a business owner/manager should not delegate.

Do not delegate a crisis. People not used to high-level responsibility are likely to freeze when the heat is one.

Do not delegate policy making. Instead, delegate policy implementation.

Do not delegate tough personnel decisions. Staffing issues are the responsibility of upper management.

Do not delegate symbolic acts. The person at the top should announce the sales records, present the awards, honor the staff and perform other duties that help unite the company.

Ten Powerful Words

"If it is to be, it is up to me."

If you are going to become a successful business owner or CEO, these are really ten very powerful words. Nothing will happen without you. New products will not be developed, marketing will not be effective, sales will not be sufficient and the bottom line will not generate profit. If good things are going to happen to your company, it will only happen if you take the initiative to make sure it all happens. You must launch the vision, outline your objectives, set the goals, and release the strategic plans. Follow-up, following through, removing roadblocks, re-adjusting and re-aligning can only come from you. Lead so that others can follow.

Chapter 5

Making Critical Business Decisions

Before you begin to think about business growth or business investment strategies, you must understand the decision-making process or risk losing what it may have taken you years to accumulate.

Decision making is an activity that cannot be avoided. It is a process we must engage in every day to function effectively as individuals. Making decisions about business affairs demands conscious attention to one's goals as well as to money.

How a Decision Occurs

A decision occurs when a judgment is consciously made after weighing the facts and examining the alternatives and their outcomes. The decision is the choice one makes from a field of alternatives. The decision is complete when it is acted upon — that is, when we do what we have decided to do (or be, or obtain, or change, or begin). Until some action is taken, the decision is not a decision; instead, it is still an idea or notion or unsettled problem in one's mind.

Decisions often must be lived with for some time; many times they have a way of altering lives, even when it is least expected. Therefore, to see how decisions operate, it may be helpful to identify some of their characteristics.

Characteristics of Decisions

1. Decisions are interrelated

A decision has a history; that is, it is related to a past and to a future. Something has occurred prior to the decision that related to it, and events will occur in the future as a result. Think of a row of dominoes standing on end. When the first domino is knocked over, the entire row falls in orderly succession. Decisions work in a similar way; once a decision is made, it sets in motion a chain reaction of further decisions.

2. Making a choice involves risk

There is no way of knowing for sure, in advance, the result of a decision. Although we may base the decision on all the facts available and obtain the best of advice, there is still the possibility that the results will not be what we anticipated. That's how most of our decisions are made; the outcome cannot always be predicted. The risks involved are often the reasons people find it difficult to make decisions, particularly big ones.

3. Decisions cause change

Although it is true that some decisions may not involve change, decisions that require the use of resources, call for change.

Decisions often require one to do things differently. If one wants to lose weight, it means a change in eating habits and regular exercise. A change in attitude usually precedes the actual decision.

Often the decision cannot be made until a change in attitude occurs that will permit one to accept the results of the decision. Many people who have stopped smoking will testify to this. The decision to stop had to be preceded by a change in attitude regarding the habit, a change that finally permitted the smoker to say, "Yes, I want to stop."

4. Decisions require commitment

A commitment is a pledge we make to another person or to ourselves. This means we agree to do something or to take some course of action. It further implies that we will accept the results of what we do as well as the conditions under which we must act. Commitment, therefore, is necessary.

When the whole notion of commitment is related to decision making, two commitments are involved:

a) The primary commitment to a goal

b) The commitment to follow through on the decision and accept the results

Consider first the matter of goals. Without a serious and determined commitment, one often lacks the incentive and courage to make major decisions related to the goal and to follow through on them. Without resolve to one's goal, the drastic attitude and behavior changes, which are sometimes needed, will hinder you at every turn.

Consider the commitment involved in fulfilling the decision and accepting the results. More often than not, a decision, to be acted upon, calls for a course of action that means work of some kind, or that alters habits, or that limits the use of certain resources (like your money).

In other words, a decision demands self-discipline. Unless there is a firm commitment to the decision, you might be tempted to throw in the towel — to give up rather than follow through.

5. Decisions involve cost

The cost of a decision may be measured in terms of money, but not necessarily. The cost may also be measured by what has to be given up as a result of making the decision, sometimes referred to as its "opportunity cost." For some people, the cost of the decision to lose weight can be measured in terms of what they can no longer eat.

Three Simple Steps

With business decisions, the cost in dollars and cents can be easily recognized. The decision-making process basically consists of three simple steps.

1. Seek alternative solutions

There is more than one way of doing things. To make a decision with some confidence, it is helpful to look at all the possible ways of solving the problem. Thus, one can better measure the resources against the alternatives and examine more clearly the possible solutions in terms of the particular circumstances.

2. Weigh the alternatives

Information must be gathered about costs and materials in order to make most decisions. The facts and information gathered are necessary so that one can weigh the alternatives. Compare the possible solutions, know what resources would be used in each case, and have an understanding of the outcomes of each solution.

All too often the alternatives cannot be judged very accurately unless more is known about them. It is impossible to decide from among several methods if one does not know what each method involves.

3. Make a choice

After studying the alternatives, you are ready to make a choice. The choice is the decision one makes after carefully examining the several possible courses of action. What one chooses will be based on personal goals and the availability of resources.

Three decisions that go into making most decisions; seeking the alternatives, weighing the alternatives, and making a choice; are each important. But until the decision is implemented, it doesn't really help solve anything.

It now becomes a matter of management; managing the resources and activities necessary to put the decision into action.

Having made a decision, one must assume responsibility for it and follow through with it. Even though there may be some risk involved in whatever is chosen, a person must be ready to accept and live with the consequences of a decision. People often spend time worrying about their choice and wondering if another decision would have been better or more to their liking.

Make a habit of not worrying whether you made the right decision. Commit to a choice and accept the result of that choice, right or wrong. To spend time second-guessing your decision only hinders your effectiveness in living with a decision. The mature individual can make decisions and put them into effect without worrying about what might have been.

The effectiveness of a decision is measured by whether or not it helps accomplish whatever one sets out to do. If the course of action chosen turns out to impede progress toward a goal, probably that choice will not be made again.

Commit to a choice and accept the result of that choice, right or wrong.

It may be necessary to stop and find out what is hindering the desired outcome. When the course of action requires more money than anticipated, another way may have to be found. Otherwise, the expense incurred may adversely affect other areas of concern.

Business decisions require specific knowledge and information. Any decision that involves the use of financial resources requires careful thought, particularly a decision that may affect one's life for a long period of time.

Decision Making Elements

Decision-making is a part of our daily lives. From the personal, to the family and on the job, each hour brings new decisions. On the personal side, decisions include what to wear, what to eat, what to speak, etc.

On the business side includes decisions about what to work on first, which meetings to attend, how long before returning telephones calls, which calls to return first, what is important in my day, which tasks shall I tackle first, etc. Accurate, intuitive and correct decision-making is crucial to every successful manager.

How important is this decision?

What are the risks in making a bad decision? What person is involved? What kind of risk is at stake? What are the financial implications of a bad decision? Ask yourself, how must time is necessary to reflect on the process before I can make a good decision.

Gather crucial information.

Don't shoot from the hip. Don't make a rushed decision unless you absolutely have to. Some problems need immediate solutions, but others can wait. Others can create false deadlines and a panicked atmosphere, but you don't have to buy into that. It's much better to weigh the effects of your decision before you make it, then to act first and think later. Make a strong effort to collect as much information as possible given your time frame for making the decision.

Strive for accuracy and consistency.

Use accurate resources. Check and recheck your sources and their sources. When gathering information it's better to listen rather than talk. Think back on previous decisions which somehow relate. Review your decision back then, compare the facts and opinions to those you have just gathered, then see whether or not there are some similarities. Does it make any sense to make a different decision this time around? If not, you make have a compelling reason to make a similar decision this time around.

Prepare a justification.

It's always good to anticipate questions before they actually occur. Be able to explain your decisions. You may be the most important person around. You may even own your own business. But don't make the mistake of thinking that your are "all-knowing." Lay the groundwork for present and future good relationships among family members, employees, peers, managers and others.

Steps To Making Good Business Decisions

A decision to finance a business, to purchase equipment, or fill a warehouse with inventory will have consequences that extend far into the future. Because of the long-range effects of many of these decisions, you need all the advice and factual help you can get.

To help make the best financial decisions, try these five steps.

1. Recall past experience

One's own experience is not foolproof, but if it is true that "experience is the best teacher," then at least you can apply what has been learned, and avoid making the same mistakes.

2. Keep good business records

Business and financial records may not provide answers to new problems, but they can shed light on how much money is available. Even the most elementary records can reveal a great deal about one's financial situation. In considering a venture that requires a financial commitment of some kind, it is necessary to know how it may affect commitments that have already been made.

From one's records it is possible to determine how much income has already been committed, how much is required for daily cash flow and expenses, and how much will be available for new business decisions.

3. Borrow experience from people you know

Often our own experience and our own records do not relate to the business problem we must solve. Other people's experience may not always suit your needs or situation, but it can suggest some possibilities and serve as a starting point.

4. Look up specific information

To find the information and knowledge you need on specific business problems, it might require several trips to the local public library or to the Internet for research on the subject. This kind of background information and understanding is essential in choosing a course of action.

5. Consult professionals and experts

Sometimes experts are not in the same professional field, but have a lot of personal experience. Other professionals are far from being experts! There finally comes a time when one must consult a professional or an expert, especially when considering financial matters.

Specialists in each field can give sound advice. Accountants, for example, are in the business of helping people solve critical and perplexing financial and tax problems. But seek several references before taking the advice of any professional!

Decisions need to be reviewed. They seldom remain fixed for all time. Just because a problem has been solved once, and the solution seems to be functioning as planned, does not mean the problem will never have to be solved later on.

Nothing about life remains static. Things are constantly changing. It is impossible to predict accurately what we will face next week or next year, and to forecast what financial problems will confront us five and ten years down the road.

To keep up with the changes in our lives, financial decisions, as well as a multitude of others, must be reviewed regularly. They must be kept in line with one's goals and circumstances.

"Journal every poor decision. Insanity has been defined as doing the same thing over and over while expecting a different result...pray before every decision. God is a good God. He wants the best for you. It is we who mess things up, not God. This is especially true in the area of decision making."

Making Good Business Decisions

Here are some great questions to ask when faced with the task of making good business management decisions.

- Are you alert to signs pointing to the need for a decision?

- Do you set aside planned time to do nothing but sort things out, think about decisions and contemplate solutions?

- Do you act or react? Are you running the business by crisis management or planned management?

- How good are you at setting priorities?

- What is your review process?

- Do you always have a backup plan of action?

- How often do you consult with others?

- Do you have a sixth sense to give gut-instinct input to your decisions?

- Can you make a quick, high-risk decision when needed?

- Do you see opportunities instead of problems?

- Can you learn from every crisis? When you learn, can you effect change?

Costs of Delay

Delaying crucial business decisions can cost you.

- Not promptly answering an inquiry can cost you a customer.
- Not properly maintaining machinery can cost you expensive breakdowns.
- Not developing new products and product lines can let your competitors have first crack at the business.
- Not improving your operations can lose you the competitive advantage you enjoy.
- Not exercising can shorten the life that you have to offer your business.

Chapter 6

Communicating With Staff, Vendors and Clients

The implementation and critical follow-though of your business vision, objectives, goals and action plans will not happen successfully without effective communication. Key participants in your business vision are your management team and employed professionals. They are the ones who must carry out your business plan. Your employees must know what role they play in the overall scheme of things and what their specific responsibilities consist of. They must receive accurate communication and have a clear understanding of what is happening.

Communication is defined in textbooks as the *"sending and receiving of information among people."* At least six messages are involved in the communication process. These six can be identified in the following ways.

- What you mean to say.
- What you really say.
- What the other person hears.
- What the other person thinks is heard.
- What the other person says about what you said.
- What you think the other person said about what you said.

Elements of Communication

*Six important elements of communicating
come in question form.*

What: What do you want to say?

Why: Why do you want to say it?

Whom: Whom are you talking to?

How: How should you best present it?

When: When should you say it?

Communication With Staff, Clients and Vendors

"It is imperative that visionary organizations cast their beliefs in such a way that the beliefs are more than just pleasant platitudes or words that sound great but have no bite. Organizations should accomplish more than just moving the beliefs from paper to people."

Some words mean different things to different people. Business relationships, which include owners, executives, managers, clients, employees, associates, vendors and competitors, are the very foundation of a firm's success. These relationships require effective communication.

Some think communication is simply starting a conversation, but many times relationships end with little more than just "talk" and the results become very expensive indeed. Instead of real communication in these relationships, talk occurs with little value.

"But missions do matter. For one reason, companies are made up of people, and people need meaning and purpose."

I called my office one day and asked my corporate finance manager for a particular figure. She gave me this number: **two-thirty-nine-forty**.... and I jotted the number down. What I had heard and subsequently written down was $239,040.00.

When conducting an in-house seminar some days later, I asked a group of my employees what these words meant to them, they came up with at least eight different answers. Two numbers given repeatedly were: 1) $230,940 and 2) $239,040. There is a significant difference in just these two numbers; a $9,000 difference! Did she say it wrong? Did I hear it wrong? Were we both right?

What did she mean to say?	$230,940
What did she really say?	two-thirty-nine-forty
What did I hear?	$239,040
What did she think I heard?	$230,940
What did others hear?	8 different variations!

It is important to ask questions or restate a point for clarification of meaning. A continuous goal should be to "say what we mean," and be sure that "what we say is what was heard." We spend almost all of our time thinking about sending information (i.e. talking & writing) in the communication process; but listening is an even more important communication skill. Listening is hard work! The brain must struggle to understand what someone is saying. One must be objective and reflective in communication behavior.

Many benefits arise from good listening skills. Listening enables us to gain work-related information. Listening enables us to be more effective in interpersonal relationships. Listening enables us to gather data to make sound decisions. Finally, listening enables us to respond appropriately to the messages we hear.

One can be a good listener by listening for the sender's central idea. This is probably the most important step in listening. To identify the sender's main idea, you must keep your own ideas in the background. If your own ideas begin to influence your listening, you may miss what the sender is trying to say. This, however, implies that every speaker does indeed have a central idea. This may be a lofty assumption to make about all communicators, but we should make it if we want to be good listeners.

Another point in listening is to concentrate on what the sender is saying. Good listening requires one to work very hard. This means developing a style of listening that enables one to get the information he/she needs, even while doing other things. Listening should be taken seriously and one should work hard to achieve it.

Our attitudes influence our listening behavior.

Sometimes we let our emotions *influence* our listening. Often we hear what we want to hear, and not what the sender intended to transmit. We often assign our own values to stimuli coming in. Our attitudes influence our listening behavior. It takes effort and practice to delay evaluation of the message until later.

It is often easy to reject what you hear as too familiar, unfamiliar, or trivial. When we hear something that is *"old hat"* to us, it is very easy to turn off the communicator because we think we have heard it before. We may also do this if something seems too trivial for us to listen to. If we are not careful, a lot of important information may be missed.

We cannot just listen for the facts. A good listener should notice the surroundings, the reactions of others, the enthusiasm demonstrated by the sender, etc. All of these peripheral signs are part of the message being transmitted.

Avoid formulating arguments against the sender's ideas before you fully understand them. Thinking up opposing arguments takes time and energy away from our primary job as listener.

Try to ignore uncomfortable surroundings. If the room is too warm or too cold; the lighting not good; the dress of the communicator not acceptable; etc. major distractions may occur.

Try to personalize the sender's topic. Be perceptive to the sender's nonverbal communication. Do not be afraid of difficult expository messages. People who are experts point out that sometimes people will refuse to listen to information they feel is too difficult or complicated. One will be successful in formulating an appropriate response only after he/she has demonstrated good listening behavior.

Look for common points of interest.

If we want to avoid potential stress for ourselves and those we're dealing with, we must consider some suggestions when we are going to be in a stressful conversations.

It is always good to look for common points of interest. If you know you're going to be disagreeing with someone, start off your discussion with some area on which you both agree. Even if it requires really digging to uncover the common ground, we should do it!

It makes a difference how you approach a person in communication. When my daughter was just a small girl, Jana, sang in Portland's Singing Christmas Tree. Her mother and I took turns getting her to final rehearsals in downtown Portland. These practices sometimes took three to four hours every evening.

One evening, while I was waiting outside in our van reading a book, a well-dressed person approached the van and knocked on the window. Since he smiled warmly, I thought it might be one of the other fathers waiting for another family member just as I was and looking for ways to pass the time. Quickly rolling down the window, I smiled and said "hello."

After exchanging greetings, I listened intently as he told of returning from California after visiting an ailing mother. He was on his way back to Seattle where he was employed by Boeing Aircraft. He indicated to me that his vehicle had broken down in Southern Oregon and he had used the last of his cash for repairs. He asked if I could spare just $28 to buy gas to get back home. He said, "Now I know this looks bad and I am totally embarrassed, but I am not a beggar."

He didn't look like a beggar; his approach was warm and friendly and he had communicated in an upbeat, positive manner. As I gave him my business card so he could send me the money back the next morning as he had just promised, I threw in an extra $32 just so he would be sure to have enough....a total of $60. That would have been the equivalent of $150 in today's purchasing power.

Guess what? He told the truth. He wasn't a beggar...he didn't beg once....he didn't have to! Because of his approach in conversation, I opened my billfold and gave him all that I had...and I never heard from him again.

Think of your own style of communication. Does it have a positive or negative effect upon others? If it is positive and rewarding, it will be the kind of conversation others want to have again and again. They will come back for more. On the other hand, if your communication with others is continuously negative, others will tend to interact with you as little as possible.

A good rule of thumb is to try to make as many of your communications relatively positive for the other person. Of course, you can't always do this because of the nature of some kinds of problems or because some other person may lack the social skills necessary to cooperate in making communication positive.

Other times, when you must take a strong position in opposition to others, positive communication may be difficult. However, over the course of your many communications with your family, co-workers and colleagues, you should be able to make the great majority of communications go easily.

Making communication positive may be difficult at times, but it comes easier with practice. Some people can keep communication constructive under pleasant circumstances, but then lose their grip on it when the pressure is on. It is an important skill to be able to put others at ease and help them stay there through the course of the communication. The stranger who approached me in my van that evening while I was waiting for my daughter, certainly knew how to put me at ease.

Maintaining Quality Relationships

Relationships that are quality require some work. Whether is be with business vendors, employed professionals or customers, your business needs relationships built on excellence. They are vital.

Here are some tips.

Care: Let people know they are important.

Hear: Listen until you understand.

Affirm: Let people know they are doing well.

Tell: Communicate clearly and be sensitive to others.

We should ask ourselves this question on occasion: *"To what extent do people voluntarily seek me out; to what extent do they take the initiative in contacting me, communicating with me, sharing ideas and viewpoints with me, and including me in their personal and social activities?"*

A flyer, which was mailed to me at the office some time ago, demonstrated how one sentence can be emphasized in a number of different ways. I saved the information but did not record its source. Here it is in summary form with my particular spin on it.

In this one sentence (a sentence containing only seven words!), there are *seven fairly obvious meanings.* The original sentence was, ***"I didn't tell John you were stupid."*** I will substitute my name, just in case your name is John.

Emphasis can also be added to more than one word in each sentence, thereby enlarging the communications problem immensely. This can be personalized by reading the following sentences aloud, emphasizing the italicized words.

I DIDN'T TELL RICH YOU WERE STUPID.

This is what is really being communicated: Someone else told him.

I DIDN'T TELL RICH YOU WERE STUPID.

This is what is really being communicated: I'm keeping that a secret.

I DIDN'T **TELL** RICH YOU WERE STUPID.

This is what is really being communicated: I only hinted at it.

I DIDN'T TELL **RICH** YOU WERE STUPID.

This is what is really being communicated: I told everyone but him.

I DIDN'T TELL RICH **YOU** WERE STUPID.

This is what is really being communicated: I said that someone here was stupid and Rich figured out for himself that it was you.

I DIDN'T TELL RICH YOU **WERE** STUPID.

This is what is really being communicated: I told him that you still are.

I DIDN'T TELL RICH YOU WERE **STUPID**.

This is what is really being communicated: I merely voiced my opinion that you weren't very bright.

My daughter, Jana, when she was in the sixth grade came into my office and recited a poem that she had just memorized. Her communication was so good, I was inspired to record it instantly. It is a poem by Shel Silverstein and recorded in the book, "A Light in the Attic." In essence, it summarizes what communication is all about.

Here it is. *"If we meet and I say, Hi, that's a salutation. If you ask me how I feel, that's consideration. If we stop and talk awhile, that's a conversation. If we understand each other, that's communication. If we argue, scream and fight, that's an altercation. If later we apologize, that's reconciliation. If we help each other home, that's cooperation. And all these actions added up make civilization."* What a great example of communication!

When presenting a message it is often more effective to choose words that are more positive in nature as opposed to putting a negative spin on the communication. By doing so, a greater chance of a positive reception is possible. Instead of saying *"why not"* it's good to say *"what if."* By *not* saying *"I hate it when,"* some conversations can be enhanced in a positive way. Try saying *"wouldn't it be better if..."*

Sometimes people use generalizations when speaking, and by doing so, sabotage their ability to communicate. To say *"he always says"* when in fact he does not always say, hurts the speaker's ability to communicate. It becomes a matter of his/her credibility.

Perhaps a way to say the same thing might be *"I've heard him say before..."* I've heard employees complain, *"Nobody cares about what I do around here"* when in fact the statement, *"Sometimes I feel like no one notices how hard I work around here,"* might be closer to the truth. Instead of supervisors commanding that it must be done *"like this,"* it might be more effective to communicate in this way: *"Here's a good idea to consider..."* or *"This may prove to be more effective."*

It is important for every person, especially those who find themselves in positions of leadership, to think about his or her communication style. I have accumulated a list of *some negative and positive communication behaviors* which can assist in thinking about one's style. It is probably a good idea to document a day of conversation to see how many of these specific behaviors can be identified in day-to-day patterns of working with others.

Negative Communication Styles

Here is a list of negative communication behavior styles, etc.

- Asking loaded or accusing questions
- Bragging; showing off; talking about self
- Breaking confidences; failing to keep important promises
- Complaining or excessive whining
- Criticizing excessively; fault finding
- Demanding one's own way; refusing to negotiate or compromise
- Disagreeing routinely
- Displaying frustration frequently
- Diverting conversation capriciously; breaking someone else's train of thought
- Flattering others insincerely
- Including changes when restating ideas of others
- Interrupting
- Joking at inappropriate times
- Keeping a sour facial expression
- Losing one's temper frequently or easily
- Making aggressive demands of others
- Making others feel guilty
- Monopolizing the conversation
- Not respecting the opinions of others
- Overusing "should" language; pushing others with words
- Overusing "why" questions
- Patronizing or talking down to others
- Playing "games" with people
- Ridiculing others

- Showing obvious disinterest
- Soliciting approval from others excessively
- Telling lies; evading honest questions; refusing to level with others
- Throwing "gotchas" at others; embarrassing or belittling others
- Throwing verbal barbs at others
- Using nonverbal put-downs
- Verbal abuse...insulting comments
- Withholding customary social cues such as greetings, nods, etc.

Positive Communication Styles

Here is a list of preferred behaviors which are more positive and will probably bring better communication results.

- Affirming feelings and needs of others
- Compromising; negotiating; helping others succeed
- Confronting others constructively on difficult issues
- Delaying automatic reactions; not flying off the handle easily
- Expressing genuine interest in the other person
- Expressing respect for values and opinions of others
- Giving one's word sparingly and keeping it
- Giving others a chance to express views or share information
- Giving positive nonverbal messages of acceptance and respect for others
- Giving suggestions constructively
- Joking constructively and in good humor
- Keeping the confidences of others
- Leveling with others; sharing information and opinions openly and honestly
- Listening attentively; hearing the other person out
- Praising and complimenting others sincerely
- Questioning others openly and honestly; asking straight-forward, non-loaded questions
- Sharing one's self with others; smiling; greeting others
- Stating agreement with others when possible
- Stating one's needs and desires honestly
- Staying on the conversational topic until others have been heard
- Talking positively and constructively
- Treating others as equals whenever possible

Chapter 7

Building Effective Teams

A "team" is defined in the dictionary as *"a group of persons associated together in work or activity." "*

Synergy" is defined as *"combined action or operation."* Applying this definition to a **"TEAM"** concept, it means that action taken among team members produces greater results than all the individuals would have produced if they had worked by themselves.

Synergism is the "something extra" that happens when a team really functions as a team...that is, when all its members collaborate; it leads to extraordinary output from ordinary people; i.e. 2 + 2 can equal 8 or 9.

The involvement of employed professionals is a vital dimension in improving quality, productivity, and profitability. Based on cooperative relationships, open communication, group problem solving, and collaborative decision making, the participation and involvement of teams of employed professionals assume a major role within an organizational structure.

Teams are not an end in themselves, nor are they a cure - all for every quality, productivity, or management problem a company faces. Ideally these teams will facilitate a process for personal growth and maturity. Some things which describe the overall purpose of the teams include:

- Encourages teamwork at every level
- Team success comes first, individual success second
- Identifies problems, proposes solutions
- Explores systems and procedures
- Discovers work simplification secrets
- Encourages participation at all levels
- Entry level people can come up with amazing ideas and solutions

Successful Teams

Teams are vital to the success of an organization and people are vital to the success of any team. Let me refer again to Larson and LaFasto's three common features of competent team members. They are as follows:

1. The essential skills and abilities
2. A strong desire to contribute
3. The capability of collaborating effectively.

Most people want to do a good job and will if properly trained and given the chance. Team members must be heard, coached, challenged and directed. People will rise to the lowest expectations of the team facilitator.

Team facilitators are not bossy, nor stubborn...they challenge people with the privilege of contribution and performance. Team members visualize what they want to accomplish, motivate each other, and work together to bring out the best in people and are team players. It is a bright day in any company when team members catch each other doing something right!

People fail in direct proportion to their willingness to accept socially acceptable excuses for failure.

It's important to have high expectations of everyone and as a team believe that each team member will be able to do an excellent job of meeting those expectations by working together. A company is successful only to the degree that it is successful at resisting the urge to be irresponsible in meeting its corporate goal.

Successful teams do not accept excuses for failure; and as individuals work on reducing our willingness to accept non-performance or failure by making excuses. Individuals could think about applying this same philosophy to their personal lives. How much more could we accomplish in our **days**, months and years both professionally and personally if we didn't accept failure or make excuses for it?

It is easy to say "I don't have the time", or "I thought someone else was going to take care of it" or "Nobody told me to do that." There are enough socially acceptable excuses to keep people from getting anything done...for the rest of their lives; if in fact this is the way a person wanted to go through life.

At most companies there are those who want to be high achievers. This can be accomplished by not accepting socially acceptable excuses for failure.

Team-building encourages personal discipline.

Individuals within a team must be open-minded. In the beginning don't expect to have a clear picture of the end result. Where one aims is seldom where he/she winds up because progress is measured with a curve. What looks like a solution today may not even be a possibility tomorrow.

Individuals should not be afraid of ignorance. All teams have to start somewhere; at the bottom or the beginning. Thinking that we know too much, may completely destroy creativity and originality. Limiting the initial amount of research and readings may help with problem solution. Trying to learn things experimentally in a team environment can also be creative.

Teams on the move are open to new ideas and enjoy creative and in-novative action. When a new suggestion surfaces, often after discussion and research, the answer is, "Let's try it out. Let's consider it from every angle. Let's present it to other teams for consideration and suggestions. What can be changed to handle it? Maybe we can improve if we use it. It's worth a test. How will it work? Let's ask our facilitator what he/she thinks of the idea. We're better than our competition. We can make it work today with a new approach. It will generate new business."

The truth is that good ideas, noble intentions, brilliant inventions, and miraculous discoveries go nowhere unless somebody forms a team to act on them. Whoever forms a team to carry out the best ideas wins. Jesus formed a team."

"Coming together is a beginning, keeping together is progress, working together is success."

◆ Henry Ford

Team Lessons From the Wild

Many species of wildlife are involved in teamwork. The geese are birds dedicated to teamwork. I grew up in rural Iowa where I have often seen them fly in a "V" formation during their migration to the South. Now living on a lake in Northwest Oregon, looking out my study window as I am typing this chapter on the day before Christmas, I am looking down on my lakeshore where I see upwards of 200 ducks and geese on my property.

Just moments ago, a flock of geese took flight in that same "V" formation that I used to see as a kid. What is not always apparent is the fact that by flying in a "V" the whole flock adds at least 71% greater flying range. This is in addition to what each bird could do if it were on it's own. If one bird drops back or out of formation - he really feels the drag of going it alone. This speaks to the truth of any company culture. By working together with a common goal through teamwork, employed professionals have a greater flying range!

As each team member works hand in hand, each will feel the uplift. A natural benefit of mature teamwork in any company is increased communication within the team itself as well as between other company teams. Teams must constantly communicate! The purpose of communication is to listen so each individual team member can learn. Team players should ask someone else to review their work and listen carefully to what is said. The point in communicating is to get new ideas that allow a person(s) to get momentum going again.

Teams must constantly communicate!

Mature teams are able to deal with problems as they are encountered, confident that their solutions would have been the same solution as management would have proposed, because both would have been made from a total client satisfaction perspective. When both employee and employer approach the daily operational problems with this central theme in mind, good team solutions become the result.

Team-building will develop harmonious manager/worker relationships; they can serve as a vehicle for the promotion of personal and leadership development; greater safety awareness should be a result; and discussion of ways to promote reduction in costs can be discovered during these meetings.

Advantages of Company Teams

Some companies have replaced departments and supervisors with teams and facilitators. What is then built are small groups of employed professionals who are involved in producing similar work. These teams meet specific objectives which include reducing errors, enhancing quality, promoting job involvement, accepting personal accountability, seeking responsibility at the grass roots level, and maturing and motivating new employed professionals.

Advantages for the company:
- Increased productivity
- Improved and more consistent quality
- Increased profits
- More loyal, responsible, and accountable employees
- Satisfied customers
- More new customers
- More repeat customers
- Better service and prices from vendors
- Greater enjoyment of profession

For the employed professionals:
- More meaningful work
- A less-stressful work environment
- Opportunity to be self-managing and have greater pride in work
- Opportunity to demonstrate creativity and innovation
- Opportunity for personal growth
- Opportunity for better pay
- Greater job security
- Opportunity to be enthusiastic about work

For the customers:

- A dependable and valuable resource
- Consistent quality and service
- An example of a responsible, ethical business
- A vendor that is interested in their success

For the vendors:

- A stronger, dependable and more stable customer
- A customer that can be trusted to practice win/win philosophy
- An example of successful good business practice
- A customer that inspires better service

Mature Teams

Mature teams show a lot of initiative.

An old story is told about four people named Everybody, Somebody, Anybody and Nobody. There was an important job to be done and Everybody was sure Somebody would do it. Anybody could have done it, but Nobody did it. Somebody got angry about that because it was Everybody's job. Everybody thought Anybody could do it, but Nobody realized Everybody wouldn't do it. It ended up that Everybody blamed Somebody when Nobody did what Anybody could have done.

Mature teams are able to ask the question, "What needs to be done and when?" Mature teams do not wait for something to happen, they make it happen. Initiative includes a lot of "preventive maintenance;" consistently monitoring all areas of the plant on a random basis.

Asking "why is this being done or why is it being done like this? Is there a better more efficient way?" Mature teams recognize when something is no longer working. They then take the initiative to correct and fix the problem. Mature teams realize that what may have worked last week and yesterday, may not be the best way today.

Maturing Teams

Team building and maturing is more effective when a group takes the initiative to plan ahead. In other words, crisis management does not work and is not effective. Teams will mature as they work together to accomplish the following guidelines.

- Respect for team players
- Match qualified persons to position descriptions
- Never add people for personality sake
- Never add bodies in an attempt to solve a problem
- Well-written position descriptions eliminate any confusion
- Appreciate people, but hold them accountable to their position description
- Evaluations are done against the position description - based on performance
- Allow people to make decisions, but make them responsible for the results
- Allow people to make mistakes, but they must learn from them and not repeat
- Recruit the best people

Productive Teams

Teams serve another purpose; that is to improve productivity. Discipline is a personal responsibility. And productivity depends upon discipline. So we can expect productive discipline to be an art we develop ourselves.

How much time could be saved and *how much more* could be accomplished if we know what to do, what not to do and what to consider before we started doing anything at all?

If we knew how to minimize failure we would be much more productive. Solving problems and making profitable decisions is simply a matter of being disciplined and observant. There is an old saying "to see is one thing but to notice what you see is entirely another."

In work groups that are involved with team building, others can observe our successes and failures and provide constructive feedback and suggestions for improvements. What we and others observe about ourselves whenever we fail or succeed in doing something is an excellent way to build an expertise on productive problem solving and decision making. Team members support each other in these areas.

Teams can help bring about that discipline in one's working environment. With the help of co-workers, one can ask questions and find answers to problems when each individual team member takes personal responsibility. It is the responsibility of each person to question all work. It is right? What could be wrong with it. How about systems and procedures? What could be improved?

Each team should pursue areas of expertise and interest because that is where the most potential to succeed lies. A key focus is to get started. Sometimes teams have a tough time with this. A philosopher once said that "words without action are the assassins of idealism." Plan ahead! Don't waste time on beautiful, in-depth plans; make them short and effective. It's too easy to make a mistake in the beginning and not realize it until the plan is put into action. Teams should plan or hypothesize a segment, then test it, then revise it. Team members should plan some more, test it again, and then try to fit the parts together to form a complete project.

Effective Teams

Quality teamwork contributes to successful businesses, projects, and the manufacturing of quality products. There is more to developing an effective and successful team than may at first be thought.

A team works effectively when its purpose is larger than the individual purposes of each of the team members.

For example, a football team's goal of winning the Super Bowl is larger than each individual member's goal of completing a successful play. In baseball it is more important to win the ball game then to hit that personal home-run!

Effective teams have a number of things in common that make them successful, goal-oriented and result-minded. Some ways to enhance this process include:

- Rewards given for collective performance, not individual performance.

- Goals are motivating, and are shared by all team members.

- Each member feels that the others are equally committed to the team's goals and objectives.

- Goals cannot be achieved by individuals alone.

- Members are able, and are allowed, to contribute from their individual strengths.

- Individual goals do not distract from the team goal.

Ineffective Teams

There are some things worth mentioning that distract from team success. Whenever something is allowed to *distract* the team from its purpose, the team becomes *ineffective.*

A few of these things include:

- Individuals do not believe in the team concept, or resent it.
- Individual power or contributions are rewarded, rather than the team effort.
- Individuals are allowed to take claim for group efforts.
- Members cannot be trusted by other group members.

Chapter 8

Essential Course Corrections

Advancing a successful business to a level of accomplishment and achievement is not an automatic given. It is one thing to start a business from nothing, but to establish a business and keep it growing is quite another. Solid growth can be tricky and stressful. Even the best laid plans can go awry.

Obviously continued growth takes a constant inflow of new ideas, new strategies and new planning. New sales come from new customers and the wants and needs of those customers are continuously shifting as their world changes.

The economy is cyclical and global business in the world is being flattened. The barriers of trade among the nation economies have been decreasing and the insourcing and outsourcing of labor, manufacturing and technology is growing at an astounding pace.

A business must be on a constant lookout for changes in the needs and wants among business and consumers as the trends of industry fluctuate without end. Strategic planning must never be set in stone and must always be adjusted and adapted to current business environment. This necessitates constant review and research that results in essential course corrections.

Jonah was a biblical character who made an essential course correction in his life. Here was an individual who got started down the wrong path and needed some adjustments to his attitude and in his personal direction.

Jonah had received a Word from God to go to Nineveh. Instead of following instructions, he heads off in some other direction to pursue another destination. He decided to board a ship in a place called Joppa and sail off into the wild blue yonder. Here's a man with Divine revelation and a clear Word from God and yet he rejects the Word and runs from it.

Jonah 1:1-3

> *The word of the LORD came to Jonah son of Amittai: "Go to the great city of Nineveh and preach against it, because its wickedness has come up before me." But Jonah ran away from the LORD and headed for Tarshish. He went down to Joppa, where he found a ship bound for that port. After paying the fare, he went aboard and sailed for Tarshish to flee from the LORD.*

Jonah's flawed decisions and the series of events which led to the need for an essential course correction.

- rejects a Word from God
- decides to go his own way
- flees from God
- boards a ship
- a great wind arises on the sea
- a violent storm arose
- the very structure of the ship is in danger of breaking up
- all the ships crew are afraid
- cargo is thrown overboard to lighten the load
- Jonah falls asleep
- sailors all cry out for help to their gods
- sailors cast lots to attempt to determine if a passenger is responsible for the storm
- the lot falls on Jonah

- Jonah admits that he serves the God who made the sea
- this revelation terrifies the sailors
- they ask Jonah what can be done
- Jonah responds by saying they can throw him overboard
- the men try to row back to shore, but could not
- the condition of the sea gets even worst
- the sailors beg God not to take their life if they throw Jonah overboard
- sailors toss Jonah over (Jonah 1:4—9)
- the raging sea grew calm
- the sailors fear the LORD
- they offer a sacrifice to the true God
- God sends a great fish to swallow Jonah
- Jonah gets to live in the fish for three days and three nights (Jonah 1:17)
- Jonah talks to God inside the fish
- he complains about the waves, current and the seaweed
- he felt his life ebbing away
- Jonah prays for deliverance and receives it
- he makes a vow to God
- he sings a song of thanksgiving
- he promises to change his ways
- God opens the mouth of the fish and Jonah is vomited on to dry land
- God gives Jonah a second chance and instructs him again to go to Nineveh
- Jonah preaches to Nineveh and all the people believe (Jonah 3:1-10)

Here is what we can learn about essential course corrections from Jonah.

- to find the right initial path we need divine revelation
- when we find the correct road, we should stay on it
- when we have a strategic plan that works, we should accept it and stay on course
- choosing the convenient or easy way is not always easy
- if we take a fork in the road we may get into trouble
- be sure you know where you are going or you may end up in a place you don't want to be
- disobedience will get you off track
- if you find yourself off the beaten path, make an essential course correction immediately
- the longer you wait to make corrections, the uglier and dirtier it will get
- we can turn our wrong choices into right choices
- God will give us a second chance to get it right
- prayer is always a good thing
- prayer can deliver us from wrong choices
- when you make the necessary course corrections, others will be encouraged
- a right attitude will keep you from making wrong choices

Chapter 9

Removing Obstacles and Roadblocks

One of the problems in the setting of goals is the failure to anticipate real obstacles. This can be caused by excessive optimism, failure to recognize alternative strategies, lead-time frames and forecasts that are missed, needed support not received, failing to foresee potential conflicts and understanding the unexpected nature of business crisis.

How does one reduce the potential roadblocks that can come your way? Here are some ways: Keep the overall aim in mind, be flexible in planning, anticipate possible schedule delays and have an alternate plan, and brainstorm in advance about what could go wrong in each area of planning.

How do you handle yourself through business roadblocks and disappointments? Character is you minus your possessions. Someone said that money doesn't change men, it merely unmasks them. Let's expand that to say business roadblocks do not change businesspersons, it reveals their true stamina.

Booker T. Washington said, "Success is to be measured not so much by the position that one has reached as by the obstacles which have been overcome while trying to succeed."

Dwight Bain said, "Major roadblocks can stop you cold. Most of these are unexpected problems that tend to change your life forever, but when you are learning to find success in any circumstance, you can make a positive change."

Character is you minus your possessions.

Obstacles to Progress

Document your obstacles.

Take a few minutes and jot down all of your current or potential business roadblocks. Categorize them in three areas. The first is those that are beyond your personal control. This could be the economic cycle of the nation or some other roadblock that you have no jurisdiction over.

The second category would be those roadblocks that are unexpected and unwanted but that if understood and dealt with immediately through corrective action, can be overcome.

The last category has mainly to do with you as a person. For example, if you have a sales organization and your primary responsibility is to bring in sales, yet you have trouble getting on the phone or making those in-person sales calls, then you have a "you" obstacle to overcome. This roadblock was placed in your path by you. It is likely a mind, emotional, or psychological obstacle.

Business roadblocks do not change the businessperson, it reveals his/her true stamina.

✓ Uncontrollable Obstacles

(Unplanned, Beyond your Control)

A. _____

B. _____

C. _____

✓ <u>Conditional / Temporary</u>

(Surmountable if Dealt With Immediately)

A. _____

B. _____

C. _____

✓ <u>Mental</u>

(Existing in the Mind, Emotional, Psychological)

A. _____

B. _____

C. _____

Adjusting to Changes

Every business requires constant adjustments and revisions to strategy. Although necessary, adjusting to periodic changes does not have to be complicated. Whenever changes are made, they too must fit within your overall business strategy.

Don't make changes just because.

Make changes that will correct ongoing problems in your company and improve its ability to carry on business within your corporate objectives and goals. Of course, the changes must be measured to see if they are producing the desired result. Anything that is measured improves. You cannot manage what you do not measure. Here are some areas of possible change and modification to both your business and personal life.

- Re-work your business plan
- Re-define your marketing plan.
- Re-define your sales plan.
- Adjust your business financial plan
- Re-focus on the client.
- Re-think your vendor relationships.
- Re-invest in personal performance.
- Re-organize work practices.
- Re-examine your organization, top to bottom, inside and out.
- Re-focus on performance.
- Re-learn teamwork.
- Reward effort.
- Re-balance your life at work and home.
- Re-learn optimism.

Sometimes roadblocks occur that require course corrections and immediate action because of "short-time" orientation. It may be that daily actions were completed and viewed on a day-to-day basis without the larger picture or end game in mind.

This would likely lead to a lack of progress toward intended goals. Perhaps it could have been prevented by asking yourself or having your key staff ask the same question at the end of each day, "What did I accomplish today that moved me forward toward a specific goal"?

You cannot manage what you do not measure.

Other times roadblocks and obstacles occur because of a lack of commitment either on the part of your staff or you. They may be focused on routine, daily insignificant activities because they are easier then doing the real work of progressing toward a business goal. If that has happened in your business, it is time for a wake-up call.

You must immediately begin to meet periodically on a regular basis to discuss potential problems and to track your progress. Set additional goals mutually, share data and progress reports, encourage informal discussion of goal progress among key staff persons, keep the entire team informed about results, progress and recognize and reward performance that meets your high development and results standards.

Continuing Your Education

Some roadblocks are encountered as the business outgrows your ability to manage it. Maybe you started out as a very small business only to see its success explode. As businesses grow, new tools and personal skills are required to maintain it.

It is important to recognize your weaknesses and take steps to fill in areas of need. Not everyone knows or has experienced everything. Although I have had a lot of hands on practical business experience, I will always have a need for further formal education.

I have a Bachelor of Science in Business and Economics with an emphasis in accounting and finance. I also have a graduate degree, an M.B.A. with an emphasis in finance and accounting. Education was a long hard row for me.

I went to school nearly full-time for over ten years while also raising a family, giving myself to charitable institutions, serving in churches and spending well-over sixty-five hours a week building and managing a successful multi-million dollar business. Looking back, it seems nearly impossible to me even now.

Many different educational opportunities are available. The choices seem unlimited. Community colleges offer on-going educational courses, one-day seminars abound, several universities offer week-long camps, etc.

If you are starting your own business, remember that ownership is not for slackards, the lazy, part-time bosses or the un-informed. Business ownership requires long hours, informed decisions and hard work. Nothing less is acceptable.

M.B.A. – M.B.O. – M.B.E.

While an M.B.A. is good education, sometimes I think another degree should be offered at our institutions of higher learning. This degree could be titled an "M.B.O." (Master of Business Ownership). It could be awarded to all of those who have started and operated successful businesses.

Or how about an " M.B.E.?" Many of us could also qualify for this. The Master of Business Experience! Whatever your level of education, don't be satisfied with it. Go to school, gain more knowledge and insight, continue your intake of learning!

Chapter 10

Implementing Necessary Changes

When necessary changes are not made, business failure is all but guaranteed. All plans need periodic changes and essential course corrections. Sometimes even well-thought out goals must be revised and changed. This may be due to changes within your industry, national economic cycles or your own business model.

You must make changes or risk financial disaster. If a plan never changes, lacks resiliency or is inflexible, it affects the company's ability to reach its long-term goals and objectives. If changes are necessary, but not implemented, goals will not be met, and wasted time will continue to be spent on unproductive tasks or activities. This continues the perpetual inefficiency of your labor expense. Your business activities will continue not matching your goal priorities.

Give constant constructive critique and feedback to regular activity not aligned with your business priorities. This will help the sincere employed professional understand what is most important in your mind. The insincere or disingenuous employee who does not align their work day with your business priorities should be encouraged to use their talents elsewhere in some other business.

Learn from your business mistakes. Failure to do so will cause them to be made again and again. Don't lose sight of your pre-determined business objectives. Don't repeat the obvious mistakes. This is a very costly way of doing business.

Following the same routine creates the same crisis. Set guidelines for improvement and create ways to learn from previous mistakes. When you come to a successful benchmark or milestone, take some time to assess what was learned and what helped the company reach that goal. Document its progress, successes and achievements.

Share the information with the rest of your staff. Always ask, "what did we learn from this experience...good and bad?" Be adaptive, flexible and responsive to changing business climates. Concentrate greatly on producing results at every level of your business organization.

Even well-thought out goals must be revised and changed.

What happens when a plan does not come together as you have expected? Maybe is was your lack of foresight and planning, or maybe the economy unexpectedly tanked. Whatever the case, you must readjust and change your plans. Some kind of change is always inevitable. Change is often necessary.

Change can be good and change can be healthy. Don't resist making changes in your business plan. Initiate change, be eager to find the better path and you should certainly not react negatively just because change is needed. When a reaction is justified, do so by rethinking, planning and then taking the appropriate action. Inaction is not the answer either.

To sit still and continue to watch a business stumble for any reason is a huge mistake. As soon as you are alerted to a problem, it's time to get it solved. Will Rogers said, "Even if you're on the right track, you'll get run over if you just sit there." In the biblical book of Isaiah 57:14 it says, "Build up, build up, prepare the road! Remove the obstacles out of the way of my people." The biblical book of Philippians speaks to those who have encountered obstacles or failures along the way. "Brothers, I do not consider myself yet to have taken hold of it. But one thing I do: Forgetting what is behind and straining toward what is ahead, I press on toward the goal...." Philippians 3:13-14

Change simply means to examine what you are currently doing to see what areas of improvement might be found. Let's pull apart the word change and use each letter individually. The letter C could represent the "challenge." What challenge, problem or need are you facing? The letter H could represent the thought of "help." What help or additional resources should you be seeking or implementing? The letter A is for "add". Is their some product, person or resource that should be added to your business?

Learn from your business mistakes. Failure to do so will cause them to be made again and again.

The letter N is for "necessary." What necessary changes should you be making right now to improve the business situation? The letter G is for "given." What area of the business should be given some most attention right now? Do you have a sale challenge? If so, go back to earlier chapters in the book and see how to create sales. The letter E is for experience. Given the experience you are now encountering, what will you put into place to make sure that you do not travel this same road again in a few months?

Many times change simply means expanded or more detailed planning. I Samuel 22:21 says this, "Go and make further preparation." Don't give up or sit around hoping for better times. Get going, make adjustments, and change the things in your business that just aren't working. Yogi Berra said, "If you don't know where you're going, you'll probably end up some place else."

There's a story about a man struggling to cut down enough trees to build a fence. An old farmer came by, watched for a while, then quietly said, "Saw's kinda dull, isn't it?" "I reckon," said the fence builder. "Hadn't ya better sharpen it?" said the farmer. "Maybe later," replied the fence builder. "I can't stop now...I got all these trees to cut down."

Insanity is often described as doing the same thing over and over and expecting different results. Be open to new ideas, learning new skills and new areas of growth. Realizing your full potential is helped by seeking the wisdom and counsel of trusted mentors.

Get buy-in from others who are involved in the decision-making process. Make sure that you are "fully buying in" on your own idea first. Realizing your full potential is taking the initiative and making a decision. Be prepared to implement your change decisions. Answer the question, "what, where, when, how, who, etc."

Often the most important area to address during time of course correction and change is your attitude. Your attitude gives you the ability to see the changes that are necessary and view them as a positive occurrence on the road to building a successful business. To change successfully, you must believe that you can make successful changes to your existing business that will get you out of where you presently are and into a brighter future.

Some people believe they are always controlled by their environment, but successful businesspersons believe they can make a difference in the world in spite of their environment. It will be hard for you to gain control of your business if you feel you are currently out of control.

Albert Einstein said, "In the middle of every difficulty lies opportunity." Voltaire notes something similar. "The longer we dwell on our misfortunes, the more we are bound by them. No rule for success will work if you do not. No matter where you find your business, or what you lot in life is, build something better on it.

Francis Bacon said "A wise man will make more opportunities than he finds." One person said that if at first you actually do succeed, try to hide our astonishment! Some people dream of worthy accomplishments while others stay awake and do them. Opportunities are usually disguised as hard work, so most people do not recognize them.

Pessimists see difficulties in their opportunities.

Optimists see opportunities in their difficulties.

Achievers are successful business people who never say these things.

- ✤ The customer didn't get back to me.

- ✤ I thought my employees were taking care of that.

- ✤ No one ever told me.

- ✤ I didn't have the time.

- ✤ But my accounts payables are not due until...

- ✤ I think things may get better.

- ✤ They said the supplies would be shipping on time.

- ✤ I'll make changes as soon as I can get to it.

Excuses are roadblocks to action.

Helen Keller said, "I am only one; but I am still one. I cannot do everything, but still I can do something. I will not refuse to do the something I can do."

In the middle of every difficulty lies opportunity

Ask the Right Questions

If you find that a course correction is necessary but you have no clue what to change to improve the condition of your business, then you need to seek help outside of your own self. That help may be close by, but be prepared to accept some of the truths that you will hear.

Ask employees:

How would you change this company if you had the power to implement any idea you have?

Ask customers:

What do you like about our company, and what would you like to change about it? Which of our products or services do you like most?

Ask vendors:

If we had to cut costs and it affected you, how would you react? Would you think of a way to work through the situation with us? How could our relationship be improved?

Ask yourself:

Did the way I conduct business today help my company? Could I have improved my performance? Am I on target to reach my long-range goals?

Even if you don't get the answers you want, asking these questions will give you some useful ideas about how to improve your business and yourself. Remember that it is not what you know….It's how you apply what you know!

Stay Focused on Your Vision

Staying focused on your vision & purpose is very key. Nothing significant is ever achieved without focus. If it's worth getting, it must be the focus of your attention at all times. Focus begins with a sense of purpose, mission and vision. This is your sense of direction, your road map, your life track. It's where you are headed.

Goals support this vision. When your vision is clear, your goals are clear. When your goals are clear, you will become more focused.

When you have a sense of purpose, when you have determined your goals for each area of life, then you need a series of action plans to pursue them. This becomes your personal strategy and tactic for achievement. This personal strategy is what you plan to do and how you plan to do it.

Don't quit. Don't give up too early.

Hang in there longer…even when you are tempted to give up. You can work through tough times and distractions.

Being focused means that you are ready and willing to commit resources, investments of time, money, effort and make other similar sacrifices to see your sense of purpose fulfilled. Are you willing to pay the price?

Becoming focused is to continue disciplined effort. This is your personal not-giving-up. Do you have the guts to remain focused, stick to your plan and pursue your goals until they have been reached? Being focused means that you must resist the temptations along the way that would keep you from continuing on. It means that you set aside all distractions that would take you off task. If your focus is clear, your goals reasonable, and your plan is sound, nothing will keep you from pushing on.

"More than 80 percent of the people who start a business fail before the business reaches five years of age. Like prospectors lost in the desert, they wander aimlessly, looking for signs of wealth. Often a single turn takes them off the path that leads to the potential mother lode."

- Don Taylor

When Failure Occurs

What happens when you start a project but it fails? According to the Naval Support Activity Mid-South Blue Jacket newsletter, a person will go through at least the following steps. First is Denial, then Anger, to Depression and finally Acceptance. They say that the word "Failure" has become a dirty word in the corporate world.

Our success oriented society often makes it difficult for those who fail to adjust. This negative attitude often forces people to take job-related failures personally, even if they had little to do with the actual events.

While no one embraces failure, some people take it harder than others, blaming themselves or others. Embarrassed to face their colleagues, unable to confide in their friends or family, they are isolated in their own hurt.

So how should one begin to regroup after failure. The Bluejacket newsletter says this.

1. Acknowledge The Failure

When this first, vital step is not taken, an atmosphere of fear is created. Instead, face your failure and see that it is an opportunity to learn and grow.

2. Seek Help To Prevent Future Failure

If you do not ask for help next time, you may not take a risk again. Not taking risks leads to stagnation and a loss of creativity and growth for individuals and organizations.

3. Failure Can Be An Opportunity To Reflect

Take the time to reflect, rethink values and interests. After reflection, make positive changes. People are often better off after they have failed, because if it hadn't been for their missteps, they might still be in the same rut.

4. See Failure As A Learning Experience

Take the time to discuss what has occurred with your associates, friends, mentors, etc. This will allow you and others to see what went wrong and how similar situations may be avoided in the future.

5. Failure May Not Always Be What It Seems

What we often label "failure" may be a normal developmental step, a shifting perspective on what is most important in one's life. The priorities that drive individuals to be corporate dynamos at age 30 may change at the age of 45, when people may find themselves more interested in family life.

"Reaching any peak in life is a result of continually improving, which is often a result of learning from failures." Todd Duncan

About Failure

Here are some thoughts to ponder...

- Learning from failure is one of the greatest gifts available.

- Look at failures, not as obstacles or reasons to give up, but as stepping stones on the road to success.

- Your future is only as bright as your mind is open.

- Success is never limited, failure is never final.

- Believe you can achieve.

- Learning from past mistakes almost guarantees future success.

- Altitude is 99% attitude.

- Success is the ability to take responsibility for failure.

- Sometimes we fail through no fault of our own...sometimes we succeed the same way.

- The past cannot be changed. The future is still in your power.

- The one thing worse than a quitter is the person who is afraid to begin.

- You can fall many times, but you aren't a failure until you begin to blame someone else.

- Forget the past! No one becomes successful in the past.

- If you blame others for your failure, do you also blame them when you succeed?

- You cannot change the past, but you can ruin a perfectly good present by worrying about the future.

- Sometimes failure is not really that at all. It may just be a result of some action or the inaction.

- When we set out to accomplish a particular feat, while we may not actually accomplish it, it may not be either success or failure. All of our efforts eventually have a result. The result may not be what we initially set out to achieve, but to make that result out as either success or failure may be to be overly judgmental of ourselves.

- While an unanticipated result may be the end of one part of your life, but it is also the beginning of another part of your life.

- If you find yourself stuck in a big hole, stop digging!

"Many of life's failures are people who did not realize how close they were to success when they gave up."

Thomas A. Edison

Mr. Edison tried several thousand different filament materials for the light bulb before he actually found one that would work. While in the process of success, its not fair to say that he failed thousands of times… he was simply eliminating all of those materials that wouldn't work.

"The brilliant moves we occasionally make would not have been possible without the prior dumb ones."

Stanley Goldstein

A Procedure for Discussing Interpersonal Conflict

There are times when essential course corrections require the solving of conflicts among staff. Unsolved communication problems are roadblocks to a successful business. Here are a few simple steps to overcome barriers in this area.

1. List the things you need to talk about.

2. Agree on ground rules.
    a. Each side will listen without interrupting while the other side presents its case. (Be brief).
    b. Each side will summarize the other's case to the satisfaction of the other, before discussion of issues occurs.

3. Person A states his case while B listens. When A is finished, B summarizes A's case in his own words. (B must keep trying until A is satisfied that B is stating things accurately, from A's perspective.)

4. B states his own case and A summarizes.

5. List any areas of agreement that may have appeared (often quite a few).

6. List any areas where you disagree and state precisely how you disagree. (Example: "A feels that ... B differs in that...")

7. Discuss possible solutions.

8. State any solutions you work out in precise from. Who will do (or not do) what, when, and where? Writing it out helps to get it clear and precise.

> *Credit: Barry C. Bartel, <u>Communication Skills and Conflict Resolution, Student Guide</u>. Faith and Life Press (1983), p. 30.*

Chapter 11

Staying Alert & Encouraged

Keeping Yourself Encouraged

It may be difficult at times to remain upbeat, especially when your business seems to be bad or going nowhere.

Discouragement affects every person at various times in the life of their business. Sometimes it is short lived, other times it seems to stay for awhile. It's not just one test that must be endured and then is gone, rather it comes to every individual time and time again. It must be faced and accepted as a common problem to all.

No doubt there is much to make people discouraged; a bad sales month, production problems, facilities problems, cash flow problems, etc. But there is no good reason why anyone should continue in a discouraged condition. Discouragement cannot be eliminated forever, but it can be dealt with in a positive manner; a manner which will encourage you and get you on track once again.

We seem to have a natural tendency to flee when things get tough. Whether it be emotional, physical, or geographical, a depressed person is likely to resist facing what may seem discouraging. Reality for him/her has become too much, and a flight from reality is the only alternative that seems open at the time.

When life begins to take pot shots at you and the bullets are coming fast and furious, you do tend to get the impression that you are being used for target practice. And yes, you do have a natural reflex reaction to run for cover. No one enjoys the assaults that life brings periodically, but *running for cover and running from the field altogether are entirely different.*

How about those times of unexpected, unplanned crisis. Crisis can crush the spirit and hope of any individual. It can make the light at the end of the tunnel seem like the headlights of an oncoming triple trailer semi-truck. But the good news is that this season of tremendous disappointment and discouragement; this event in our lives that has a crushing affect upon our spirits can be a temporary factor in your life.

In the midst of the crushing...in the dream shattering, there can be a refining of our lives that serves as a purifying process that may not have happened otherwise. Sometimes seemingly brutal blows and bruised spirits can lead to a softening and a penetration of tough minds and cold hearts.

There are probably many experiences that can trigger discouragement. It might be a friend that let you down, a marriage in disarray, a rebellious child, an unfinished task, a mistake in your past that just won't go away, an unachieved plan in your life, a habit which you cannot seem to break, a severed friendship, a broken home, an untimely death, the loss of a good job, an unfulfilled romance, a lingering illness or a disappointment that just happened. Discouragement comes in all shapes, sizes, and times.

Yet it is very seldom that it is caused by any one incident in particular. Perhaps more often than not it can come about by a number of small things which begin to build stress into one's life and can even be triggered by an emotional down or when one gets run down physically.

It is status in our society to rush day after day and to always be in a hurry. We rush to work in the morning, hurry home in the evening, scamper over to the supermarket for a few groceries, cram as many errands into the remaining time and "cheat our bodies" out of the proper rest and relaxation properly due them. Everything seems to be too important to leave until the next day. It's got to be finished today!

Now that I've touched on the problem of discouragement, what can we do to lift ourselves out of it. Here are a few suggestions for you to consider.

1. Take care of your physical self.

Inadequate rest, nutrition, exercise, emotional strains we bear each day, and problems that come our way all contribute to a physical condition which gives easy vent to times of discouragement. Thus part of the antidote to discouragement is to restore physical vitality.

A well-balanced diet along with physical exercise promote good health. Burdens to healthy living such as late night activities, crisis living and tension-filled personal relationships must be abandoned. The intricate relationship between the physical and the emotional is not yet fully understood, but is not to be taken lightly.

2. Maintain a positive attitude

Life gives to us "reality checks." There is nothing like an unexpected sickness or physical impairment that gets our attention. During a weekend on the Oregon coast, I severely damaged my right knee. The impairment ended after surgery to correct multiple problems and a year of physical therapy. Still other complications arise from time to time as a result of the original injury. I found while lying in the hospital bed, that reality never takes a nap. During this season of intense discouragement, I learned to appreciate other parts of my body that were still working well; hearing, sight, etc. This helped the discouragement to leave and helped clear my emotional roller coaster.

Moments of discouragement are a part of normal life. Of course it hurts when something wanted does not materialize. We might as well admit that those disappointments affect us. But the end of the world has not come. All of the problems will pass with time. However, just how quickly the problems go away seems to be dependent, at least in part, upon our attitude and how we deal with the unpleasant events of life.

> *Knowledge is advantageous, skill is indispensable,*
> *experience is invaluable, communication is fundamental,*
> *enthusiasm is beneficial, initiative is essential, but*
> *ATTITUDE makes the difference.*
>
> Rich Brott

If we allow ourselves to become depressed and our spirits to take on a negative outlook, discouragement will ride us week after week. On the other hand, a good positive approach to life will knock the blues out of the way before it has a chance to gain a strong hold.

Have you ever blown it big time? Did you make a bad business decision? A lot of our mistakes and problems are brought on by ourselves. Often when we are about to blow it, we begin to make excuses. We justify our ways and methods, usually with the best of motives. We become pretty good salespersons. In fact we're so good, we may not convince others, but we can do a snow job on ourselves!

Mistakes are made. Mistakes do happen. But sometimes they could have been avoided; maybe not at that moment, but in circumstances leading up to it.

Optimism reflecting a positive outlook on life will help one to deal effectively with discouragement. One who sees only the dull, the drab and the dreary is at peace neither with him/herself nor with the world. His/her trouble is probably in untrained and wayward emotions.

As soon as he/she gets up in the morning, the fault finding begins; the weather, the person next door, the bacon & eggs, the newspaper headlines, the boss at work, and anything else that comes to mind.

If you are this kind of a person, think about getting more sleep so you feel cool, calm and collected when first awakened each morning. Then resolve to start the day right; beginning with an attitude adjustment of optimism and cheerfulness.

3. *Peace can come through understanding.*

A sense of understanding can sometimes bring inner peace during periods of discouragement. If, a teacher or a parent does not understand children, they can wear on his/her nerves and continue to frustrate to no end. As a business person, you can be a careful planner, take great care in your marketing program, and yet still fail to see the desired increase in sales. These events can seem like mountains during times of personal stress. A little understanding can ease the tension considerably. Perhaps your marketing plan was just fine. There may have been other circumstances outside of your control that led to a reduced sales month.

4. *Make a commitment to assist others who are less fortunate.*

Unselfishness has a way of minimizing the blues. Stop thinking about yourself and how you feel each hour of the day. Start thinking of others and remember the responsibility and privilege of making others happy. The moment you think of how to increase the joy of others, your own level of happiness will rise. The less you think about yourself, the less depressed you will be and the more inner peace you will enjoy.

It is healthy to develop the habit of doing something for others as you begin each day. There is no one so busy that he/she cannot squeeze in a good deed for another. It may be only to wish someone a good day or to inquire concerning his/her health and prosperity.

Even a smile at just the right time may enrich a life more than you may think. Congratulate the person in the office who was promoted to the job that you wanted so badly. Compliment the janitor, the grocery clerk and the postman for the fine service they are giving you. All of this helps to forget about our own discouragement and at the same time brightens the day for others.

5. *Become an encourager.*

Some individuals are very self-conscious and do not excel in meeting new people. Friendliness can put these individuals at ease and provides relief in an uneasy situation for them. Think about how much it does for you when someone takes the time to smile, shake hands, say Good Morning, nod, introduce themselves and be friendly. It is an art to have the ability to put someone at ease...but an art that can be learned.

If you are sad, sorrowful or despondent, a smile brings cheer. If you are in a situation where boredom seems overpowering, there is nothing like a firm handshake and a nod to bring a positive spin to the atmosphere.

It can be stimulating and invigorating. Be friendly! Make it a point to brighten up someone's day! You'll see a frown turn into a smile. Gloom will give way to cheer and what's more, you will become revived and rejuvenated yourself.

It seems that when one needs encouragement the most, for example after a personal failure, the human tendency is to disapprove, discount and add to the discouragement. How opposite that is to becoming an encourager!

The only difference between us and them is circumstance. We need to reject the opportunity to kick a person when he/she is down. People in need are an easy target for lingering depression. Discouraged people never need more critics. There already exists plenty of stress, self-criticism and a whole lot of hurt. So when someone is hurting and discouragement prevails, it's time for some major support.

Gold is a precious commodity that is very expensive even by the ounce. Not everybody has had the opportunity to inherit precious jewelry or family heirlooms. But there is something much more valuable than any of these things. It is the ability to uplift and encourage others! Genuine heartfelt, warm-hearted encouragement reduces material possessions to mere things. And look at the results. Think of the good you can do when it is needed the most.

Don't allow life to become negative! Stop looking at dark clouds and rainy skies. Look forward to the bright and sunny ones. When strong adverse winds blow, the clouds will soon disappear and the sun will shine again.

Getting Rid of Stress

Here are some ways to reduce your stress.

- Be positive

- Eat healthy foods

- Enjoy relationships

- Exercise regularly

- Form good habits

- Get adequate rest

- Help someone in need

- Reflect and re-adjust

- Schedule time to relax

**Each evening before you go to bed, turn your worries over to God...
He's going to be up all night anyway.**

Vital Energy

When you get rid of stress, you can gain a new outlook on life and enjoy revitalized energy.

There are four kinds of energy that you need in abundance.

◆ Physical Energy

for purposes of endurance

◆ Mental Energy

for problem solving

◆ Emotional Energy

motivates the use of physical & mental energy

◆ Spiritual Energy

makes you feel fulfilled, useful, a sense of purpose, produces drive, inspires others, etc.

The quality of your effectiveness depends upon the degree to which you are able to cultivate all four forms of energy.

Controlling Your Workplace Emotions

Blowing up in anger at your business is a sure way to lower your credibility in the eyes of your employees and customers. This kind of behavior tells people that you're not in control, you're not strong - even that you're unstable. If you're a volatile type, first examine the things that trigger your anger.

Some of the most legitimate common triggers may be:

- routinely or unfairly receiving criticism
- being ignored or not taken seriously when discussing projects or giving instructions
- being lied to, lead astray, or given skewed information
- experiencing continual unscheduled interruptions
- working with background noise in a fast-paced environment

Some of the most non-legitimate common triggers may be:

- not able to accept other perspectives
- personal problems not related to work
- a tendency to "fly off the handle" before getting complete information
- a failure to see the entire picture
- inability to work with conflicting personalities

If you have trouble identifying your anger triggers, try to journal the cause or surroundings leading up to time of anger. This can be used to identify common threads which might be a trigger point that one can avoid in the future.

Once you understand what your particular triggers are, deal with your anger using one of the methods below or design your own way to get a handle on your emotions.

1) Give no reaction at all.

Look strong in the midst of the situation, and either deal with the agitator in private or later vent your feelings to a non-business friend.

2) Count to 10;

Count to 10 and then, speak in a slow, reasonable, calm voice. Make the other person strain to hear you. It will put him or her off guard and you will appear to be a model of self-restraint.

3) Make light of it.

It can help diffuse a tense situation. And sometimes when you take a different point of view, you see that anger isn't called for.

4.) Remove yourself,

Remove yourself, if possible, from the situation as soon as allowable; i.e. short walk, break, etc.

Emotions at work can be unavoidable at times. But if you want the respect, even admiration, of your employed professionals, you must learn how to control them.

Dealing with Business Worry

What should you do when business seems bad? What is your reaction when a plan does not seem to come together? Do you regroup and begin again, or do you get depressed, begin to worry and wonder about everything? Worry accomplishes nothing. Worry is the opposite of faith.

A Christian businessperson cannot be filled with faith and worry at the same time. The psalmist David had plenty of times when he could have been filled with worry…even to the point of wondering if his enemies would kill him. Even Jesus taught us to ask for our daily bread. He is more than willing to provide for us but apparently is very adamant that we ask for his help first.

God never abandons His children. He always provides for them. In His time, God will always right the wrongs, avenge injustice and keep His promises.

God will provide for you through many natural resources available to Him. In addition to the ongoing natural resources that He has placed on the earth, when desirable He will provide for us through supernatural means. He fed the prophet Elijah with food sent by ravens. He fed the five thousand men plus women and children from a few meager morsels of food.

When we were children, we never worried about our parents providing for us. My parents provided me with a warm bed, daily food and a roof over my head. Nothing was left to chance. In this manner our Heavenly Father provides for our needs daily. Day after day, month after month He proves His love for us even knowing our needs before we ask Him.

Matthew 6:34

Therefore do not worry about tomorrow, for tomorrow will worry about itself. Each day has enough trouble of its own.

Acts 14:16-18

"... he provides you with plenty of food and fills your hearts with joy."

Psalm 37:25

I was young and now I am old, yet I have never seen the righteous forsaken or their children begging bread.

Matthew 6:8

Do not be like them, for your Father knows what you need before you ask him.

1 Peter 5:7

Cast all your anxiety on him because he cares for you.

Psalm 37:3-5

Trust in the LORD and do good; dwell in the land and enjoy safe pasture. Delight yourself in the LORD and he will give you the desires of your heart. Commit your way to the LORD; trust in him and he will do this:

Psalm 115:12

The LORD remembers us and will bless us:

Proverbs 3:5

Trust in the LORD with all your heart and lean not on your own understanding;

Jesus compares our need for faith and trust in Him and suggests that we learn a lesson from the birds. The birds are not lazy by any means. They do search for food, they dig their worms, they snatch bugs, they build nests, they work hard and are very productive. Yet the Scripture says that it is God that feeds them.

Matthew 6:26-27

Look at the birds of the air; they do not sow or reap or store away in barns, and yet your heavenly Father feeds them. Are you not much more valuable than they? Who of you by worrying can add a single hour to his life?

This is the story told about a man who had a need. It is a rather fun tale, whether true or not.

There once was a man who had nothing for his family to eat. He had an old shotgun and three bullets. So, he decided that he would go out and kill something for dinner.

As he went down the road, he saw a rabbit and he shot at the rabbit and missed it. Then he saw a squirrel and fired a shot at the squirrel and missed it. As he went further, he saw a wild turkey in the tree and he had only one bullet, but a voice came to him and said "pray first, aim high and stay focused."

However, at the same time, he saw a deer which was a better kill. He brought the gun down and aimed at the deer. But, then he saw a rattle snake between his legs about to bite him, so he naturally brought the gun down further to shoot the rattle snake.

Still, the voice said again to him, "I said 'pray, aim high and stay focused." So, the man decided to listen to the voice. He prayed, then aimed the gun high up in the tree and shot the wild turkey. The bullet bounced off the turkey and killed the deer. The handle fell off the gun and hit the snake in the head and killed it. And, when the gun had gone off, it knocked him into a pond. When he stood to look around, he had fish in all his pockets, a dead deer and a turkey to eat.

Matthew 6:28-31

And why do you worry about clothes? See how the lilies of the field grow. They do not labor or spin. Yet I tell you that not even Solomon in all his splendor was dressed like one of these. If that is how God clothes the grass of the field, which is here today and tomorrow is thrown into the fire, will he not much more clothe you, O you of little faith? So do not worry, saying, 'What shall we eat?' or 'What shall we drink?' or 'What shall we wear?'

In the above verse, Jesus has each of us take a look at the flowers of the field.

Matthew 6:27

Who of you by worrying can add a single hour to his life?

Then finally Jesus sums up the entire address on the subject of worry by showing us the futility of spending time with worry. Why worry, when you can pray? Worry about nothing, pray about everything!

Matthew 17:26

So go down to the shore and throw in a line, and open the mouth of the first fish you catch. You will find a coin to cover the taxes for both of us; take it and pay them. TLB

One of the wonderful principles of the Bible is that of divine supply; God promises to supply our every need. Financial supply is a God-given gift. God gives us many gifts, but His greatest gift was His death on the cross, providing a living sacrifice for our sins. He has given us the gift of salvation. He gives us the gift of life, of family, of friends and of good health. The Bible says that He loves to give us good gifts.

Matthew 7:11

If you, then, though you are evil, know how to give good gifts to your children, how much more will your Father in heaven give good gifts to those who ask him!

If a gift is promised, but not yet given, why do some people borrow and go into debt just to obtain what God had intended to supply anyway? Is this because of our impatience or a lack of trust? Is it because we don't really have faith for God's abundant supply or don't agree with His timetable?

When two people marry in the traditional Christian wedding, the vow includes the statement, "until death do us part." Many good marriages break apart because of a great wall of financial miscommunication. Unfortunately, in our current culture, this sacred vow might be more accurate had it said, "until debt do us part." Many statistics now conclude that the majority of all divorces are influenced by financial controversy and seemingly insurmountable debt.

1 Kings 17:15, 16

So she went away and did according to the word of Elijah; and she and he and her household ate for many days. The bin of flour was not used up, nor did the jar of oil run dry, according to the word of the LORD which He spoke by Elijah. (NKJV)

Supernatural business provision happens when the natural is not enough.

If we can make it happen on our own, there is no need for faith. No need for trusting God. And it follows that if we do not have faith and have no need for God, He will not step into areas we have reserved for our own self-control. The principle of supernatural provision is that He is strong when flesh cannot be.

Philippians 4:19

"And my God will meet all your needs according to his glorious riches in Christ Jesus."

Notice that the scripture does not say the local banker or loan officer will supply your needs. Nor does it say that the welfare department of your government will supply your needs. It says that God, and no one else, will supply your needs. God is your only Source! It's not your business that provides your income. It is God who provides your needs. Is it God's business or your business. Where does the ownership fall?

This story has been told for many generations. It is about a Christian family that was going through some tough times. They were so destitute that they didn't even have food for their next meal. The father and mother got down on their knees and cried out to God for food so their children would not go hungry. A man who was not a Christian was walking by their house and heard their prayer. Instead of feeling bad for them, he decided to play a trick on them.

He went down to the grocery store and bought a huge box of groceries, put it on their front porch and rang the doorbell. When the Christian parents saw the groceries on the porch, they immediately began to thank God for it. Just then the unbeliever walked up and said, "Why are you thanking God? I'm the one who placed the groceries there." The Christian father replied, "Oh no, it was God who answered our prayer and provided the groceries. But I do want to thank you for being His delivery boy and bringing them to us!"

God is your sole source, your only provider. Through Him and Him alone are all your needs met. Your professional employment is just that, it's not an end-all. When the economy tanks, so do jobs. When the industry sector that employs you goes bust, your job disappears with it. Don't trust your education, don't trust your experience, don't trust your business; trust God.

In the natural economy, we experience such things as debt, bankruptcy, recession, depression, and other financial crises. But in God's economy there is no such thing as want, lack, recession or depression. Yet because most of us are not aware of God's economy, and His willingness to provide financial abundance, we need to be strengthened in our faith when it comes to the area of finances.

God reveals His economy by taking a "little" and turning it into "much."

The most obvious example is the miracle of the feeding of the five thousand in Matthew chapter 14. This is where Jesus took the little boy's lunch of five loaves and two fishes, blessed it, broke it, and distributed it to His disciples, who fed five thousand men, plus women and children.

Many of us, as a matter a fact, find it hard to believe that God is interested in such practical things as finances. Yet Bible scholars tell us that one out of four of the teachings of Jesus is related to our material possessions. In God's economy there is no such thing as want, lack, recession or depression.

Another example is found in II Kings, chapter 4. This is a story from the life of Elisha the prophet, who gave instructions to a widow who had a need. Her late husband's creditors were about to take her two sons as slaves. She sought help from Elisha, who instructed her to collect empty jars from her neighbors, and then go home and pour oil into the jars from the one jar of oil she had.

She left him and shut the door behind her and her sons. They brought the jars to her and she kept pouring. When all the jars were full, she said to her son, "Bring me another one." But he replied, "There is not a jar left." Then the oil stopped flowing. She went and told the Elisha, the man of God, and he said, "Go, and sell the oil and pay your debts. You and your sons can live on what is left" (II Kings 4:5-7).

Besides the fact that God took a little and turned it into much, we should also note that the size of the widow's blessing was dependent upon her expectancy. In other words, how much oil she received depended on how many jars she collected—the more jars, the more oil. When she got to the last jar, she probably wished she had done a better job of collecting the jars.

- God knows your business need.
- He wants to provide for your business.
- He desires to bless you with good gifts.

Everything we have is a gift from the Lord. He desires to bless and prosper you. Jeremiah 29:11 says, "For I know the plans I have for you," declares the LORD, "plans to prosper you and not to harm you, plans to give you hope and a future."

Chapter 12

Effective Time Management

I will be taking considerable time and writing much on this timely topic. If you cannot discipline yourself to use your time efficiently and productively you will never be a successful businessperson. Time is a very valuable commodity. God blesses individual effort.

Advancing a successful business requires efficient and productive use of our time. We are required to redeem the minutes and capture the hours. We should be filling efficient days and occupying industrious weeks. Our effective and productive months should result in progressive years. We have a responsibility not to waste the precious little time we have been given.

Several years ago, I traveled to a small town with a couple of friends. Our mission was to paint the house of a dying man. The house was in need of a fresh coat of paint and we were wanting to pay him a visit. Instead of just standing around watching his pain, we intended to help brighten his day by painting the house.

As we were saying our good-byes at the end of the day, he made a profound statement I still remember as if it were yesterday. He said, "It pays to give it all you've got while you're on stage, because you never know when your act is up." Soon afterward, he died of cancer. And since that event I have lost many close friends to various illnesses. I often have wondered, why them and not me? Some of the finest Christians I have known, have been taken pre-maturely. While we certainly do not have the answers to these tough situation, we do know that time is a heavenly endowment.

Time is our tool. It is a wonderful gift. We should not be a slave to it; we should put it to proper use as an investment for the future.

"It pays to give it all you've got while you're on stage, because you never know when your act is up."

God is the giver of life and the giver of time. He has the right to expect us to use it wisely. We have a responsibility to make the most of it. Good stewards of time and finance are not only faithful and responsible, but also have an honesty and financial integrity about them.

God is the God of the past, present and future. He has no time constraints. He is not bound by the limitations of time. Time means nothing to Him. See what the Word says about it.

2 Peter 3:8

But do not forget this one thing, dear friends: With the Lord a day is like a thousand years, and a thousand years are like a day.

On earth, we (you and I) are constrained by time. Our lives are but a few years, at best. Our time is limited. Time means a lot to us. God has allotted us just a limited amount of years and, therefore, is very concerned how wisely we spend those years.

Job 14:1, 2

"Man born of woman is of few days and full of trouble. He springs up like a flower and withers away; like a fleeting shadow, he does not endure."

Psalm 90:10

The length of our days is seventy years — or eighty, if we have the strength; yet their span is but trouble and sorrow, for they quickly pass, and we fly away.

Ephesians 5:15, 16

Be very careful, then, how you live — not as unwise but as wise, making the most of every opportunity, because the days are evil.

John 9:4, 5

As long as it is day, we must do the work of him who sent me. Night is coming, when no one can work. While I am in the world, I am the light of the world.

Time is valuable and utterly irretrievable; it is a priceless commodity. Suppose your bank credited your account each morning with $86,400.00, carried no balance from day to day, and allowed you to keep no cash in your account. Then suppose every evening the bank canceled whatever you failed to use during the day.

We all have this kind of bank; its name is time. Every morning it credits us with 86,400 seconds. Every night it considers lost whatever time we have failed to invest for good during the day. It carries over no balance.

It allows no overdrafts. Each day it opens up a new account. Each night it burns the records of the day. If you failed to use the day's deposits, the loss is yours.

We are all given 1,440 minutes each day, 168 hours each week. This makes 52 weeks each year for which we must account. In spite of its value and unique characteristics, we probably waste time more thoughtlessly than anything else.

Adlai Stevenson once said, "It's not the days in your life, but the life in your days." In other words, it's not how much you do that counts, it's how much you get done that has purpose and lasting benefit.

This seems to be the great paradox in life. We generally feel as though we don't have enough time, yet we have all the time there is. Time is NOT the problem; the problem is how we use our allotted time.

"It matters to God how we use our time. Our affairs are His affairs. It doesn't mean we are slaves to unpleasant obligations. Even Jesus rested and went to places apparently for enjoyment." Max Anders

- Time is our tool. It is a wonderful gift. We should not be a slave to it; we should put it to proper use as an investment for the future.

- Most of us would never think of going through life without budgeting and investing our finances. Yet, most of us waste a great percentage of our time. It is just as important to study the stewardship of time as it is to study the stewardship of our finances.

- Money can be spent, or it can be invested. The same is true of time. To invest either is to use them in such a way as to bring future benefits.

- The benefits of investing time are often realized later in time -- usually when time has become a scarce commodity. Time carefully planned and invested will rarely be wasted.

- People sometimes say that "time passes." But in reality it does not. We go by. Time stands still. Time does not help a person to help themselves. It is how we use the time that is allotted to us that really counts.

- In time management, all roads lead to the management of self. Often we say, "I wish I could manage my time better." What we should really be saying is, "I wish that I could manage myself better!" The management of our time and ourselves takes perseverance and self-discipline, but no investment pays higher dividends.

Managing Yourself

Self Management is another word for Time Management. Everyone wants more time. Give time to some people and it's like giving too much candy to a small child....they get into trouble real fast and it can become a disaster. For others, more time or better time management becomes a great asset to them and their business. Note the following guidelines with respect to the management of one's self and time.

- If you do not respect your time, no one else will.

- Everyone has the same amount of time. Some use it wisely, others waste this precious resource.

- Using time is a matter of choice. Some choose to use it wisely and accomplish great things. They invest in their pre-planned goals and objectives. Other choose to invest their time in areas of minimal return.

- You can work hard or work smart. Actually, you should first work smart, and then work hard. While working hard can be an admirable quality, it is not enough. Working smart is knowing what to do and what not to do. It's fairly easy to know which projects need your attention, but it is harder to know which ones you should not be spending time with.

- Beginning each day with reflection and answering the question, "What do I want to accomplish today, instead of what do I need to get done today" is not only wise but imperative. There is an "attitudinal" difference in the two questions. The first question is proactive and the second is reactive. With the first, you attack your day. With the second, your day attacks you. Who's running whom? Are you calling the shots, or is the day running you? Do you run your business or does your business run you?

Controlling Your Life

❖ Not having control of your life can cause you to have a negative outlook on your environment and yourself.

❖ Having control of your life can cause you to have a positive outlook on your environment and yourself.

❖ The degree to which you feel you have some control in life usually is the degree to which you feel positive or negative about your future.

❖ Control begins with your thoughts. You can have complete control over this area. How you think about your circumstances or any given situation determines how you feel. How you feel determines your behavior. Self-discipline, self-control and self-management all begin with taking control of your thinking and thought life. Eleanor Roosevelt once said, "No one can make you feel inferior without your consent."

❖ Different seasons in our lives, some circumstances and certainly many situations we find ourselves involved in, can cause us a lot of stress and unhappiness. When you find yourself in unpleasant environments, you can take some action. First of all, you can move forward and do something to change it. You can take hold of the situation and make it different somehow. Secondly, you can simply walk away from it. Sometimes you regain control by letting go of the person or situation and by getting busy reaching toward something else; another goal, another project, another customer, etc.

❖ Keeping in control is the result of good choices and wise decisions. This is why it is so important to know your purpose in life, the goals you wish to achieve and having a plan of action for reaching those goals. You must know what it is exactly that you want out of life; how you will serve your purpose. One of your main responsibilities in life is to get control of it. This sense of control becomes your foundation for building greater happiness and success in the future. Be sure of your purpose. Make sure it's rock solid.

Choosing Between Commitments

A great part of time management is choosing correctly between commitments. More important is choosing what to commitment to and what to set aside. Where are you going to spend your precious time? Here are some serious questions to consider.

✓ Is This Important?

✓ Does It Focus On My Purpose?

✓ Will It Help Achieve One Of My Goals?

✓ Is It An Immediate Priority?

✓ Why Is This Important?

✓ Why Should I Get Involved?

✓ Is Now The Proper Time?

Did You Know?

How are you spending your time? It is estimated that in the average life of 70 years, time is used up as follows:

- 3 years - education

- 3 years - reading

- 3 years - convalescing

- 4 years - conversation

- 5 years - transportation

- 6 years - dinner table

- 8 years - amusements

- 14 years - work

- 24 years - sleeping

Making a "TO DO" List

One of the most effective time management tools are "TO DO" lists. I use several of them, depending upon the general category that I need a list for. Here is why they are so effective.

- They create a systematic framework
- Your day becomes organized
- Deadlines that are crucial can be met
- It can be a designation to others what is most important
- It enables you to be very productive
- It helps you resist unimportant interruptions
- High-priority tasks get done first
- Your personal or internal communication is put to paper
- Your mind is always clear on what must be done
- It helps you pace your time better
- Procrastination is avoided
- Productive hours are within your grasp
- Significant progress can be made without being a workaholic
- Start to finish - the day can be logical
- Unnecessary worry is brought to a halt
- You can take it with you during the day

Personal Time Assessment

What do I wish I had more time for?

_____

_____

_____

_____

_____

_____

_____

_____

What would I like to spend less time on?

_____

_____

_____

_____

_____

_____

_____

_____

What would I like to have happening in my life that is not happening now?

_____

_____

_____

_____

_____

_____

_____

_____

Take Time

Time management requires that you appropriately balance your obligations. Schedule in important personal time.

TAKE TIME TO WORK

-- it is the price of success.

TAKE TIME TO THINK

-- it is the source of power.

TAKE TIME TO PLAY

-- it is the secret of youth.

TAKE TIME TO READ

-- it is the foundation of knowledge.

TAKE TIME TO WORSHIP

-- it is the highway of reverence that washes the dust of the earth from our eyes.

TAKE TIME TO ENJOY FRIENDS

-- it is the source of happiness.

TAKE TIME TO LOVE

-- it is the one sacrament of life.

TAKE TIME TO DREAM

-- it hitches the soul to the stars.

TAKE TIME TO LAUGH

-- it is the singing that helps with life's loads.

TAKE TIME TO PLAN

-- it is the secret to investing your life in things that make a difference.

■ Author unknown

Analyzing My Typical Work Day

- What went right today?

- What went wrong today?

- What time did I start my top-priority task?

- What patterns can I see from my typical day?

- What habits must I clearly change?

- What was the least productive period of my day?

- What was the most productive period of my day?

- Who caused my interruptions?

- What caused my interruptions?

- What activities needed more time today?

- What activities could I have spent less time on today?

- What activities could have been delegated? To whom?

- What could I have started on earlier in my day? How?

- How can I eliminate my three biggest time wasters?

Controlling Your Time

Control your time! Don't be controlled by others. Many people are controlled by the events and activities of others. They are always running to the drum beat of another.

Charles J. Givens, author of SuperSelf: *Doubling Your Personal Effectiveness* (Simon & Schuster) gives us a strategy for the successful use of time. He says to ask yourself *"Do I"* questions. They are:

"Do I...."

- Plan my daily objectives and activities?

- Prioritize my daily activities?

- Show up on time?

- Start on time?

- Refuse to get drawn into confrontations?

- Eliminate interruptions, even from friends?

- Separate my emotions from events?

- Maintain a positive, "can-do" attitude?

- Plan my work, then "work my plan"?

- Complete my day by prioritizing for the following day?

Time Management Involves Activity Planning

- Identify specific activities

- Set priorities for activities

- Estimate the time needed for each activity

- Schedule the activity

My Unproductive Activities

✓ _____

✓ _____

✓ _____

✓ _____

✓ _____

✓ _____

✓ _____

✓ _____

✓ _____

✓ _____

✓ _____

✓ _____

✓ _____

✓ _____

✓ _____

Getting Control of Your Time

The most important thing a business owner or manager can do is to get control his/her time. Disorganization, feeling overwhelmed, finding too little time to do too many things, being over-extended, etc. are all areas that relate to each other. If you find yourself in this category, here are some tips to help you get back in control of your time:

◆ **Choose.** Choose your critical chores and obligations. Set a time frame. List items to be accomplished by lunch, and then those things which should be done in the afternoon. Stick to your list.

◆ **Perform.** Complete just one item at a time. Don't jump around from one uncompleted task to another. You'll relieve tension as you finish each item. A sense of accomplishment will counteract your sense of being overwhelmed.

◆ **Spread.** Don't spread yourself too thin by trying to do too many things at once. You must set priorities for each day and, if necessary, each hour. Get the most important things done first.

◆ **Delegate.** Convince yourself that it's not necessary to do everything yourself. You can still be certain that things are being done the way you want them to be when you delegate.

◆ **Pass.** Pass on work that limits the time you need to finish your major responsibilities. Learn to say "no" to requests. You can't say "yes" to everything without spreading yourself too thin. Decide what you must do -- and want to do -- and say "no" to all other requests. Allow yourself to say "no" to the tasks that will cause you to fall further behind in your primary duties. Your customers, associates, and superiors will understand if you explain that other work is more critical at that moment. Offer support and assistance, but pass on the request unless it is more important than your current task.

◆ ***Prevent.*** Prevent burnout and frustration by setting a steady pace. Sometimes a regular pace that allows for some accomplishment is better than a faster one that makes you spin your wheels. Time management is a critical skill for continued success. Everyone has the same amount of time. Don't spend yours treading in circles that turn your days into zeros.

◆ ***Telephone.*** Don't be a slave to the phone. Have others screen your calls. Use an answering machine when you don't want to be disturbed. Schedule a telephone hour to return all calls.

◆ ***Avoid.*** Avoid all of those terrible time killers. Telephone interruptions, drop-in visitors, and meetings are common time wasters. But indecision, procrastination, and a lack of self-discipline, as well as boredom, frustration, indifference, and resentment, are the most damaging time killers.

◆ ***Procrastinating.*** Don't do it. Get those unpleasant chores done first -- if they're important. Divide large tasks into smaller ones. Set reasonable deadlines. Reward yourself when you accomplish something.

◆ ***Clea***n. Clean your desk. When was the last time you actually saw the top of your desk? If you have a problem keeping track of things, projects, papers, lists, etc. than you need a cleaner desk, cleaner files and some organization in your life. A poor system (messy desk, cluttered files, etc.) for organization will rob you of efficiency, waste your valuable time and hamper your ability to serve customers well. Use an "in-basket." Make everyone use it. Don't let them dump on your desk, chair, etc. Empty your "in-basket" once each day.

◆ ***Paper.*** Get rid of it! Some paperwork can be delegated. Status reports, general inquiries, research, etc., can often be completed by someone else. Let them! Much of your "In" basket should be going "Out" to your associates. For involved projects, delegation is essential. Break up larger segments into smaller segments and let someone else complete the task. Do the final compilation and analysis yourself -- but not the initial leg work.

Other paperwork can be dumped immediately. Just because it is addressed to you does not mean you must keep it. Use the trash can or recycling bin liberally. If you can't see any immediate use for the information, get rid of it. If the paperwork that comes across your path cannot be delegated or dumped, then just do it!

File it, route it, place a phone call, whatever seems necessary, but do something and get it out of your life! If you can't complete the project associated with a particular piece of paper, label a file folder, place it in your drawer and make a note to yourself. It is better to have one list than several stacks on your desk, chair, bookcase, and floor, etc.

Controlling the volume of paper is the first step to getting organized. It will help you to do your job better and more efficiently.

Daily Analysis

This is an overview of a typical work day for me.

Job Activity	Priority	Estimated Time	Actual Time

Job Activity	Priority	Estimated Time	Actual Time

Plan Your Work

Detailed planning is absolutely necessary. With proper planning you can gather the necessary materials, systems and procedures and utilize spare moments for the preparation of coming events. Planning for five or six days helps you realize how your work fits into the overall weekly picture. This takes the rush out of life by giving you time to fit your priorities into a manageable weekly schedule. Plan your work. Get it done!

G – *Goals*: When planning your week, ask these questions. What are the goals and objectives you would like to accomplish this week? What results do you want to see by the end of the week? Write them down and rank them by importance.

E – *Events*: What events must take place this week in order to achieve your goals? List the necessary events and activities and put them in the order or sequence in which they will occur.

T – *Time*: How much time will it take for you to complete each activity? To plan realistically, allow yourself more time than you think you will actually need. This builds in a certain amount of flexibility if unexpected problems develop.

Look at your calendar and determine when you can do each activity. Most people underestimate the power of a schedule. But rarely does anything get accomplished without scheduling specific time for that event to occur.

I *"I" Discipline*: Get yourself going. Decide that "I will" follow my schedule this week. "I will" stay to complete the events and activities as I have planned. "I will" be persistent. "I will" complete my weekly objectives.

T – *Task*: Stay on Task! Don't get discouraged. Focus, Focus, Focus!

D - *Divide & Conquer*:   Break big jobs into small parts and complete the entire job by working on one piece at a time.

O - *One*: Do only one job at a time. Finish it, then tackle the next one on your list.

N - *Never Give Up*: Keep plugging away each day of the week -- even if you get sidetracked. If this happens, get back on task and start with the next event. Some time may be lost, but the sooner you begin again, the more productive the week will be.

E - *Expect the Unexpected*:
Interruptions are common. Increase your time margin. Some say to add at least a 10% fudge factor to every appointment.

Dealing With Too Little Time

What can you do when you run out of time? Are there some options to consider? Yes there are....consider these.

Working Faster:
............*often produces more problems*

Working Longer:
.... *results in physical & mental fatigue*

Getting Organized:
..............*some definite value*

Making Choices:
..............*for the best results*

Wrong Criteria For Allocating Your Time

What should your priorities be?

Here are some typical problem areas.

- We want to do the easy jobs before we do the difficult jobs.
- We begin projects we have resources for.
- Unplanned tasks come before planned tasks.
- Things we like come before things we do not like.
- Projects which we can complete faster get our attention first.
- Demands by others get our first response.
- Socially expedient activities come before urgent needs.
- Missed or approaching deadlines demand our response.
- Fun tasks come first.
- Interesting projects grab our first response.
- Tasks that provide immediate closure get our attention first.
- Arrival order is how we determine our workday.
- Response is on the basis of the one who wants it.
- Small jobs are tackled first.
- Habit determines our day.
- Consequences, good or bad, determine what we give our time to.
- Crises and the so-called emergencies of others dictate our day.
- Random selection gets us involved in the day.

Successful Time Management

Making the most of your day is very important. It requires your day to be very efficient and productive. That is not always so easy. Everyone experiences "time robbers" -- defined as inefficient meetings; procrastination; a disorganized desk; interruptions from the telephone or unexpected guests; failure to plan ahead; or numerous other unplanned uses of your time.

These "time eaters" waste your time at the office causing you to fall behind on your work or at least prevent you from being more productive. They can rob you of your personal time also. You can make the best of these unforeseen circumstances and reclaim precious lost hours by managing your time in a realistic and productive manner.

Each of us has exactly the same 24 hours in the day. Successful people manage their time. They set priorities and then allow their priorities to manage their calendar. Ineffective individuals are often mastered by the loudest voices, the urgent and the unplanned. They are ruled by pressures, not by priorities. Most people find time management troublesome because they don't understand the basic principle of time. People react to circumstance by being controlled -- ideally, they should control circumstance.

Think of time as your personal resource and you will be more likely to use it wisely. It you think of it as a valuable and scarce resource, you will most likely take steps to prevent its wasteful use. If you "blow" a day, it's gone. You can't save up time -- if you waste time, you also waste opportunity. The key to managing your time is developing the philosophy and the habits that put you in control of your life.

A person must know his/her purpose for the week, month and year. The ability to know just what one must accomplish in any given period of time is the very essence of time management. Having a clear sense of purpose or vision of what you must accomplish is the first step. Knowing this, one can then evaluate every event, every activity and every conversation and determine whether or not it moved you closer to your goal.

Having determined your purpose for a larger period of time, you must have a clear idea of its effect on the present day. What are the things that I need to be involved in today that will fit into my overall purpose. Once you know how today fits into your larger plan, make simple daily plans. This can be accomplished through simple lists of attainable daily goals. Take each thing on your list one step at a time. Point all of your conversation, events and personal efforts toward that direction.

Don't try to do everything at once or you'll wind up not completing anything. It is impossible to focus on all that you must do in a given year, month, week or even a day. Some people get little accomplished in a given period of time because they are unable to get focused. Unorganized people usually fall far short of their potential in life, because they are often unfocused, overextended and constantly facing multiple challenges.

It has been noted that animal trainers carry a stool when they go into the cage of lions. Why is this? The trainers always have their whips and pistols at their side for protection. But according to some, the stool is the trainers' most important tool. The trainer holds the stool by the seat and thrust the legs toward the animals' face. The animal apparently tries to focus on all four legs at once. In the attempt to focus on all four, a kind of paralysis overwhelms the animal, and it becomes tame, weak and disable because its attention is fragmented.

Focus on one activity at a time.

A simple formula for getting organized is this: Focus on one activity at a time. In order to determine what that activity should be, three questions need to be asked before picking from a wide array of possibilities. First, how important is this task? Second, how urgent is it. Third, will focusing on this task take me closer to my predetermined, balanced, personal-family-job purpose and goals?

At the end of the day, review your progress. Did you get it all done? Did you accomplish a significant amount? If not, what were the events that hindered your progress. Are you closer to your weekly & monthly goals as a result of your efforts today? Effective time management should not be about scheduling every minute of every day. It's not about lots of diaries and time logs. It is about using your time to accomplish what is most important in your life and in your profession.

Author and lecturer, Steven Covey, had the following observations about what it means to be a successful person. He said that successful people lead "balanced" lives. They read the best literature and keep up with current events. They are active socially, having friends. They are active intellectually. They read, watch, observe and learn. Within the limits of age and health, they are active physically.

They have a lot of fun. They enjoy themselves. They are secure and have no need to brag, drop names or borrow strength from past titles or achievements. They are open in communication, simple, direct, non manipulative. They tend to understate rather than to exaggerated. They are not extremists.

They do not make things all or nothing, good or bad as either/or. They think in terms of continuums and priorities. Their actions and attitudes are temperate and wise. They are not workaholics, fanatics, crash dieters, pleasure addicts or martyrs. They're not slavishly chained to their plans and schedules. They live in the present, carefully plan the future and adapt to unexpected changes. They are willing to admit and then forget mistakes.

Some people become slaves to time. Balance is the key. Some weeks in my life, it seems every minute of every day and night are totally taken up with things that do not necessarily bring me closer to my purpose and goals, either professionally or personally.

I find myself doing some things just because others expect it of me. Just how many social activities can one attend? How many errands must be run that others could do for themselves. How many meetings require your attendance that could be avoided, or even done away with altogether. Are you caught up in time gridlock? If so, here are a few tips:

Decide what you want out of life. Assess all of your activities. If they add significantly to your life keep them. If not, dump them.

Understand your limits both physically and mentally. Don't take on more than you can handle. It's not necessary and not life changing. If you burn out sooner, you'll be of no help to anyone later.

Build cushions of time into your schedule. If you don't, you'll end the day/week/month/year out of breath, out of energy, out of focus and maybe even totally burned out. Reduce the daily tension, and increase your effectiveness by prioritizing what is really necessary in today's schedule. Find a slower pace. Some people are addicted to rushing; rushing here, rushing there, etc. Know the difference between necessary haste and pure impatience. Before you commit to a new activity or involvement, subtract an old one.

Prioritize Lists

When prioritizing your day/week/month/year, ask yourself this question. "What do I want to accomplish by the end of the period?" After a period of time has come and gone, what do you want to see? I like to prioritize my list in this fashion. I label it "NIP." When it comes to those things which would demand my time and attention, I "NIP" it.

1. Necessary -   task must be done
2. Important -   task should be done
3. Possible -   task worthwhile

Each night , write down three or four tasks from your necessary folder. Keep the list handy. Try to complete as many of these as possible the very next day.

Do Related Jobs Together.

Each time you change to a different type of work, your mind must change gears. Sometimes as much as 20 minutes can be required to make that transition. When you do work that has related aspects together, you cut down on transition lag. The more related characteristics that tasks have in common, the greater the benefit of grouping these types of work together. Group your telephone calls to avoid having an entire day punctuated by endless telephone interruptions.

Keep a Clean Desk

Get rid of any paperwork that you do not use on a daily basis. Store it, drawer it, or toss it. Too often, incoming and outgoing mail gets thrown into one pile. The result? Complete chaos. Designate a specific desk space or bin to keep incoming mail until you have time to deal with it. For outgoing mail, set up another bin where it is easily visible as you leave your office or work area. Work from a clean desk. Clutter is not only distracting, it makes it too easy to lose things.

Paper Handling

In an ideal world, the only papers on your desk would be those you are working on. But most of the documents on our desks need to be filed, copied, tossed or routed elsewhere. Handle each paper only once if at all possible. Separate your papers into folders, based upon the importance to you. Or simply organize the papers in stackable bins labeled TO FILE, TO COPY and TO ROUTE. Then, of course, there is the wastebasket -- don't be afraid to make use of it.

Continuously refine what goes on top of your desk. Don't use the desk as a perpetual filing cabinet. Clean up your desk each evening before leaving the office. You'll find it much easier to get a productive start the next day. Nothing can seem as overwhelming as clutter when you arrive to work in the morning.

Use the Circular File

Use your wastebasket! Don't bother to open mail that you didn't solicit or mail unrelated to your business needs. I save at least ten to fifteen minutes a day by not opening mail that doesn't affect the way I do business. Hundreds of pieces of mail -- which will not prosper or help the operation of this business -- come to my office each week. To sort through it and open it just because it arrives at your desk, is to waste literally days out of every year. Watch your fax mail and e-mail also. Don't feel obligated to open it just because it shows up!

Do a Clean Sweep

Periodically, clean up areas that are no longer necessary. These include computer files, paper files, marketing brochures, catalogs, etc. There are any number of reasons for discarding an item. If that piece of paper does not require any action on your part, toss it. It probably exists elsewhere. If it is outdated, get rid of it. If it is just "miscellaneous" information for possible consideration later, dump it. Believe me, if it is important enough, it will show up again. Cleaning up the physical clutter in your life will also serve to clean up the items cluttering your thought processes. Keep the clutter out of your life!

Management Tools

Despite the availability of many great organizational tools, many people still don't complete their projects on time. Even a simple "to do" list won't work unless you take the time each day to keep it current. Organize with time management tools only if you will continuously use them. All kinds of sophisticated tools are available for purchase, but if you don't use them or rely upon them, they all are worthless. The simplest tool is a piece of scratch paper and a pencil. But if you don't turn that into a "to do" list and use it daily, even it will not help you get organized. Successful time management today means finding a system that works for you. Each person is different, and no one system will work well for everyone.

Organizational Strategies

When choosing organizational methods, there is no right or wrong approach. It really doesn't make much difference how you do it; the most important thing is to do it continuously and in a consistent matter. The purpose of an organizational strategy is to order your personal time and life. If you constantly feel "cluttered," out of time, and out of control, some sort of organized effort must be subscribed to in order to put you back on top of matters. Organization by itself has no value. But when it helps to put you in control of your life so that you can be an effective and productive person, it becomes very valuable to you personally and to those whom you serve.

Work Hard in Prime Time

Every person has a prime time, slowing down time, and lag time. Prime time equals your biggest energy burst, your premium benefit; so push the work out! Lag time means that you're slowing down. So take some time to relax. Work at a pace that is comfortable for you, but work consistently all day long…you'll get more done.

Analyze Your Time

Time is a tremendous resource available to all of us. Since it is perishable and irreplaceable, it is important to analyze how we spend it. Is it spent in productive ways, or is there a lot of ill-spent time within our schedule? Occasionally spend some time tracking your activities. How much time is spent in travel that could be avoided? Could you make four stops in one trip instead of making four trips with one stop each? How much time do you spend sitting in lobbies, waiting for appointments, or listening to unscheduled guests?

If these things cannot be avoided, involve yourself in productive paperwork or reading instead of just waiting while the time passes. Measure your time for a few days, weeks, etc. Analyze how you spend your time. Note problem areas and create a time management procedure that increases your productive time. Be committed to improving your time management skills.

A Special Day

Declare a personal "Get It Done" day. This might help you to finish the little unpleasant or boring tasks that you have been carrying around on your "to do" list for some time. Let's face it; we all procrastinate. On a daily basis we put off whatever we don't want to tackle, doing only the tasks that we like and absolutely must take care of. But then all of those odds and ends pile up until we begin to feel pressured to get them done.

Having a monthly "Get It Done" day could be the time to finish just one bigger task or several smaller projects. You might clean the garage, clean out your office desk, update computer files, or reorganize and update your contact or address list. Make note of this special day in your daily planner -- you'll find it easier to get it done.

Saving Time

Instead of inviting people to your office, visit them. That way you can leave when you're ready to end the meeting. Arrange your office so you don't face the door. If you don't make eye contact with people who pass by, you can avoid some unnecessary conversation. Stand up when a visitor enters your office...and stay standing. If you don't invite people to sit down, the business will get finished sooner.

When someone interrupts your work, let the person know you're willing to talk -- but not indefinitely. Tell the interrupter that you must be back at work on your project by a specific time. When conversations turn to social topics, bring them to a close. This doesn't mean you should be anti-social; just save the socializing for lunch and breaks.

Over-Commitment

The great coach of the Green Bay Packers, Vince Lombardi, once inspired his football team in this manner. While discussing the impact of exhaustion on human courage, he noted that, "Fatigue makes cowards of us all."

What a profound and exacting message he had. How often have you been overworked, over-tired, and found yourself beginning to whine, gripe, blame others, or verbally hurt those you love, simply because you have tried so hard to please others by giving your time and resources? When a person is "over-committed" he or she is no fun to be around. When over-fatigued, and feeling the pressure to produce in those moments when you should be resting or even sleeping, a time of reflection may be in order.

The time has come to stop kidding yourself; this hectic pace is not simply a temporary problem – it's probably a habitual lifestyle that you have learned. Time usually proves that the rush is never over. One thing leads to another and the temporary pressures gradually develop into a long-term lifestyle. Don't let it continue to happen! Learn the secret of living one day at a time. Everything does not have to be done today.

Workaholics, like myself, push themselves to get everything done today. Guard against over-commitment. Don't let others program your life so that you consume your last ounce of energy and use up all the free moments in the day. Learn to say no gracefully but firmly. If you happen to be a workaholic, develop the capacity to do nothing. sometimes the body has more sense than the mind. Pay attention to it. Learn to say no. be stingy with your time.

Post Your Goals

Put both your long-range and short-range goals in writing. It's difficult to hit a target you cannot see. The goal-setting process alone is practically a guarantee that you will achieve greater results. Post your goals. Goals that are out of sight are out of mind. Encourage yourself and others to be prepared to present an abbreviated version of their goals on a moment's notice. Each day, ask yourself: What have I done today to bring me closer to achieving my goals? This discipline keeps the pressure on you to be more goal oriented.

Delegate

Successful leaders don't try to do everything themselves. However, they do make sure that it does get done. You may not be the best person to get the job done. Sometimes others can get it done quicker, better, and more accurately than you could have. Don't be afraid to delegate.

Convince yourself that it's not necessary to do everything yourself. You can still be certain that things are being done the way you want them to be when you delegate. Create a communication record for each subordinate. Record each item you delegate and the deadline that was agreed to. List each item you plan to discuss the next time you sit down together. Follow-up and keep your staff accountable.

Become a Dictator

How many things have you forgotten to do because you didn't jot them down when they came to mind? Purchase an inexpensive "Voice It" recorder. Save time by recording all letters, memos, or ideas that pop into you mind. Your dictation skills will increase with practice.

Don't Procrastinate

Get right on all of those unpleasant chores. If they are a priority, do them first. Divide the larger tasks into smaller ones. Reward yourself when you get a few of the tasks accomplished…take a quick walk, grab a cup of coffee or tea, have a snack, etc.

Mark Twain is credited with saying this, "The secret of getting ahead is getting started. The secret of getting started is breaking your complex overwhelming tasks into small manageable tasks, and then starting on the first one." I concur!

Schedule Personal Quiet Time

Schedule quiet time. Deep thinking can only occur during quiet time. Inform everyone around you about the period of time in which you are not to be interrupted. Block out time to dream, plan, review goals, review purpose, etc. Schedule it in your weekly calendar just as you would any other important appointment.

Extended Time

You can add thirty minutes to each day by rising just ten minutes earlier, lunching just ten minutes less, and retiring just ten minutes later. This will give you an extra 183 hours per year. If dedicated to a specific project or goal, (reading to your children, writing a book, enjoying a hobby, prayer and meditation, etc.) think of what you could accomplish each year.

Control the Telephone

The telephone is a tool. Don't let it become a thief of your time. First of all, don't mix working hours with personal business. Keep yourself on task during your work day and keep focused on the business of the day.

Secondly, don't let others waste your time whether it be personal friends or other unsolicited calls to your office. On any given day, at least ten or twelve calls come in for me which are screened out by our receptionist.

Additionally, some calls get through after telling the call screener that I am expecting their call or they are returning my call. When the caller begins his/her "canned solicitation," I immediately hang up. There is no need to be polite since he/she got through to me by not telling the truth to the receptionist or in some other devious way.

If a call comes through when you are unavailable and is not urgent, schedule a part of your day for returning calls. This will enable you to concentrate on more pressing matters at hand without having to start and stop the same project multiple times during your day.

One day when I was away at a much needed seminar, I returned to my office at the end of the day to find 48 different paper messages on my desk from people trying to speak with me. This was in addition to the voice mail, cell phone and 200 email messages that I received on that day. Control the telephone, screen your calls, and focus on the core business of your position. If you do so, you'll get a lot more done!

Learn to Say "No"

If something doesn't fit with your goals, objectives, plans, priorities or service to others, learn to say "NO." You cannot say "yes" to everything without spreading yourself too thin. If you give yourself to many things at once, none of the tasks will be done with accuracy and completeness. You must set priorities for each day and, if necessary, each hour. Get the most important things done first. Decide upon what you must do in order to fulfill your business and personal responsibilities and "just say no" to all other requests.

Do the Right Things

Peter Drucker says, "Of late I've been doing less but achieving more."

Form habits which do the right things. Habits are first formed by the activities in which we participate. After formation, habits then form us and our present and future. Not to consciously form good habits, is to unconsciously form bad ones. No habit is an automatic action nor is it an instinct. Habits do not just happen, they are caused. Habits are acquired reactions to previous choices. If you can determine the original cause of a habit, it is probably within your power to change it.

Do you want to be successful in the management of your time? Forming habits that benefit your personal and business goals will help you achieve success. People who fail often times have formed habits that "do the wrong things." Sometimes success or failure in life begins with early habit-forming choices. The harvest that we reap in our lives can often be measured by the attitudes and habits which we cultivate.

Value Today

We tend to categorize time in three areas: Past, Present, Future. While we can learn from history, we cannot change it. It is gone forever. It no longer exists. While we can prepare for the future, it is yet to occur. We cannot use future time. This leaves only the present moment available for our use. Only today... this hour, this minute is available to us. Only the present moment truly exists. Now is the moment to make the best use of our time. To think that "tomorrow" will be better than "right now" is wishful thinking.

Do what you can do to properly use the time available to you now. Now is the appointed time, use it wisely. Even if the day starts out wrong, don't give up on it. Rethink, retool, regroup, and turn it into a productive event. Forget about discouragement caused through lost time or unexpected events. Make the best of what is left in the day. Nothing is worth more than this day. Today's actions will determine tomorrow's achievements.

Don't get caught in needless conversation

If you find yourself caught up in needless conversation, get out of it quick! Simply state the obvious -- you have to get back to work. Peers often need someone to take the lead and break it off . . . or even better, not allow it to get started.

Work smarter, not harder

When inventing the light bulb, Thomas Edison made some 8,000 attempts. Most of us, like Edison, will have periods in our life when we won't be able to function in the most efficient way. But the most important step is to get started. If you don't get started, you can't get it done.

Learn to rest creatively

The mind and body soon tire of working at one type of job or in one place or position. Fatigue begins to set in. Frequently all that is needed is a momentary change of pace. Sometimes you can take five minutes to think through a program or read an article and then return to the task at hand.

The "To Do" List

Rewrite your "to do" list daily -- always keep it current. Revise it at the end of the evening before you retire for the day. List the jobs that need to be done that very next day. Number them in the order of their importance. Then, visualize the materials that these jobs will require. Subconsciously, you will begin to prepare for the many tasks that will require your attention the following day.

Prioritize your "to do" list. Before you begin each day, review the "to do" list to determine which items can be delegated. Of the items not delegated, discipline yourself to do the most critical activities, first by numbering each item from most to least critical. Be sure to get numbers 1-10 behind you before moving on to 11-20. A daily "to do" list is a must. A weekly "to do" list is advised. A monthly "to do" list will help you stay on track.

Review Your Agenda

Leave enough time at the end of your day to review what you've planned for the next one. Think about what you'll need tomorrow. Prepare yourself physically and mentally. At the end of the week, verify scheduled appointments and prepare your strategy for next week.

Establish Weekly Objectives

Know what you are trying to accomplish with your life and determine how this week will help you accomplish those goals. Leave your week, month or year to chance and chances are you won't like the way your life is lived. Write a general priority list of all projects and deadlines and assess the importance of each. This will guide you to get priorities completed first.

Develop a Regular Work Schedule.

Many people hate to be tied to a regular schedule. Some may even feel that it cuts down on their spontaneity and creativity. With the help of a schedule, however, you will find that you have less resistance to difficult jobs and are mentally prepared for each task. Set appointments, schedule phone calls and allow time to complete projects.

The most important thing is to have a clear idea of your priorities and to spend as much time as possible on your high-priority items. Record your goals in a daily planner that contains a prioritized list of objectives. Update the list and check off items as they are finished.

Chapter 13

Resisting Organizational Procrastination

What does it mean to procrastinate? Procrastination means doing low-priority activities rather than high-priority ones. An old proverb says, when all is said and done, more is usually said than done. To procrastinate means to put off doing a task -- for no good reason. Impel yourself to get it done. Be tough on self-discipline.

Most procrastination is the result of irrational thinking. You talk yourself into putting off a task, not because it is simply unpleasant, but because it is awful, horrible, UNBEARABLE! Convince yourself instead that the task is worth doing, even if it's hard getting started.

Challenge your excuses for putting the assignment off. For example, if you generally excuse yourself by saying, "But I work so well under pressure," argue that "working under pressure really leaves me harried and tired, and I don't have the time I need to be creative." This type of inner debate can keep you from stalling and works for any excuse, not matter how "logical."

Don't let procrastination be a pleasant experience. If you usually procrastinate by socializing, don't socialize. If you must procrastinate, do it in unpleasant conditions. Lock yourself in your office. No coffee. No visitors. When the fun goes away, the procrastination just might disappear.

Confirmed procrastinators usually work in a feast or famine pattern.

One way to fight the tendency is to schedule frequent tasks for regular times. Dictate letters and memos between 9:00 and 9:30. Return telephone calls between 11 and 12 every morning.

Procrastination is an emotional problem.

Let's take a close look at your habits.

- What things do I tend to put off the most?
- What things am I currently delaying?
- Do I know when I am procrastinating?
- What negative things happen when I choose to delay?
- What positive things happen when I choose to delay?
- How do I feel about my procrastination?
- What causes my procrastination?
- What can I do to overcome my problem?

Are You a Procrastinator?

Here are some questions to ask yourself.

Do I . . .

- Put off doing something I have to get done?

- Wait to move until someone forces or strongly encourages me to do something?

- Look for reasons (or excuses) not to do something I should do?

- Fail to complete projects I've started?

- Allow myself pleasant indulgences (oversleeping, overeating, skipping responsibilities)?

- Find that I've run out of time to complete a project properly because I didn't start soon enough?

- Allow obstacles and difficulties to prevent me from completing a project?

If you answered "yes" to some of these questions, you should develop some time management strategies. Consider these thoughts to get you going.

- Ask yourself, "What is the best use of my time at this moment?" Then, just do it!

- When you kill time, just remember it has no resurrection.
- Unsuccessful people are ruled by pressure. Successful people are ruled by priorities.
- The easiest way to start a project is to "start a project."

Chapter 14

Implementing Business Productivity

To implement is to put into practice, to put into service, and to put into operation and action all of the strategic planning that has already been carefully done. All the planning in the world comes to naught if the plans are not executed.

Execution must be prompt and done in a competent, efficient manner. Implementation of your business plans must be carefully prepared so that all of your accumulated strategic work and effort gets off to a great and proficient start.

Where are you going from here? What are your current initiatives? What combination of labor, resources and ideas constitute your vision for the next big advance? What transitions must you undertake to insure a successful future?

It is not enough to have a business strategy. You might have the best laid strategic plans, but if they are not implemented, you still have nothing. Your business success and success in advancing your enterprise remains solely at the door of implementation and execution of those plans.

Successful Business Implementers

- The have a predisposition for action; they get the job done.

- They accept 100% of the responsibility for results.

- They are courageous and risk takers.

- They are spiritually aligned.

- They are functionally focused; they know where they are going and how to get it done.

- They are highly decisive; they move things forward continuously.

- They are impeccably honest.

- They are inquisitive; they don't get lazy mentally.

- They are intensely goal-oriented.

- They are persistent and committed.

- They have a sense of urgency; they get more done, and on time.

- They have above average ambition.

- They have above-average will power.

- They have purpose; and seek to fulfill it.

- They have tremendous desire; they look at the reward not the challenge.

- They welcome evaluation and assessment.

Advancing Forward by Reviewing the Past

While we often read of current examples and revere those with whom we are familiar to glean insights into expanding our business, it can be very beneficial to look back into the past and read the historical and biblical accounts of men and women who successfully faced similar challenges and overcame them. Let's recount the story of Nehemiah,

Nehemiah Prepared for Implementation

Nehemiah held the prestigious and very influential position of the king's cupbearer. He served King Artaxerxes and had his trust. He generated a strategy to plan, organize, mobilize and implement great resources in order to rebuild Jerusalem.

Nehemiah implemented strategy in this way.

- he heard about the status of Jerusalem and responded with prayer and fasting (Nehemiah 1:1-11)
- a time away from the king is sought and a return time set
- the king's service is left for a period of time so Nehemiah can help rebuild Jerusalem (Nehemiah 2:6)
- Nehemiah sends out the clarion call to the people and motivates them to service (Nehemiah 2:12-20)
- Israel begins to rebuild the walls of Jerusalem
- Nehemiah deals with the discouragement of the workers
- Nehemiah plans a prayer of "revenge" so the walls cannot be destroyed so easily (Nehemiah 4:4)
- the enemies of Israel try to ambush Nehemiah to get him away from Jerusalem ((Nehemiah 6:3)

- detailed planning resulted in a secure wall built in just 52 days (Nehemiah 6:15-17)

Here is what we can learn about planning from Nehemiah.

- prayer and fasting should precede all planning or undertaking
- when are doing kingdom service, we have God's blessing on all that we do
- discouragement is a common problems that can be overcome
- we must resist any obstacles that may come our way
- planning means that there is an understanding of everyone's responsibility
- good planning means that every person has an important role
- excellent planning and implementation results in solid gains
- we can be attacked in the implementation stage long before we really get started
- people who are following the plans must focus on getting their part done
- there should be no distractions to the plan until the project is completed
- good planning equals great achievement and become a testimony to what can be accomplished with a God and man partnership (Nehemiah 6:15-17)

Business Planning

"Plans fail for lack of counsel, but with many advisers they succeed".
Proverbs 15:22

Business success is always the result of a lot of planning, intense work, good habits and continual follow through. We are what we repeatedly do. Excellence is not an act but a habit. In fact the only place that you will find success before work is in the dictionary. It is a planned event and rarely happens without great personal effort. God can bless our productivity, but cannot bless the habits of a lazy person.

Success comes in cans. Failure comes in cannots.

Philippians 4:13 says, "I can do all things through Christ who strengthens me (NKJV).

Another great Scripture which talks about blessing those who are productive is found in 2 Corinthians 9:8-10. "And God is able to provide you with every blessing in abundance, so that you may always have enough of everything and may provide in abundance for every good work. As it is written, "He scatters abroad, he gives to the poor; his righteousness endures for ever." He who supplies seed to the sower and bread for food will supply and multiply your resources and increase the harvest of your righteousness." (RSV)

Implementing Business Productivity

Good business stewardship is not merely an occupation or a profession, rather it involves being productive. In Jesus' parable of the talents in Matthew 25, the stewards reported their earnings. One servant, however, merely hid his entrustment, and earned no increase – he lost his portion. The faithful ones not only had increases but also, received more because of their faithfulness.

Excellence is not an act but a habit.

From the very beginning, God commanded creation to be fruitful. God is energetic, creative and imaginative, and is the life giver. Business stewards or managers are to be concerned with productivity and so cultivate God's creation to be productive.

It is a privilege to live in a productive society. Productive societies are composed of many productive individuals. When my days are full of productive tasks I enjoy life. My normal going-to-sleep activity is to close my eyes and mentally survey all the productive things I accomplished during the day. If I have had an efficient and industrious day, I fall quickly to sleep.

A warning about being productive is seen in Jesus' story about the unfruitful branch of His kingdom, which He says will be cut off by the husbandman (John 15:1-5). God wants to have a productive Kingdom and stewards who will be faithful.

As good business stewards, we are required to work hard. If you work for someone else, you need to do it with everything you have. Give more than is required; go the second mile and the third and fourth. Proverbs 6:6-11 says, "Go to the ant, you sluggard; consider its ways and be wise! It has no commander, no overseer or ruler, yet it stores its provisions in summer and gathers its food at harvest. How long will you lie there, you sluggard? When will you get up from your sleep? A little sleep, a little slumber, a little folding of the hands to rest and poverty will come on you like a bandit and scarcity like an armed man."

Check out the ant. The ant has no one to tell it what to do – no supervisor, nor overseer, and yet it is a self-starter, a self-motivator. The ant works all summer long gathering food for the harvest season. The Scripture extends a wake-up call to the sluggard hoping for some kind of response. It says to the sluggard, "Have you not slept enough?" "How long can you possibly sleep?" "Do you want to go hungry, do you want to go through life looking for handouts because you have not the where-withal to earn your own keep?"

Scriptures on Productivity

Matthew 17:27

"…go to the lake and throw out your line. Take the first fish you catch; open its mouth…"

We are to take action; be proactive. The abilities and giftings that He provides motivate us to action. Sometimes it takes our persistence in doing the same things faithfully with the heart of a servant. Other times, it is useful to try new things or new methods and seek after new opportunities. Sometimes it is the steady plodding that brings the success of the blessed life.

Ecclesiastes 9:11 says, "The race is not to the swift or the battle to the strong, nor does food come to the wise or wealth to the brilliant or favor to the learned; but time and chance happen to them all". Hebrews 12:1-2 advises, "…let us throw off everything that hinders and the sin that so easily entangles, and let us run with perseverance the race marked out for us. Let us fix our eyes on Jesus, the author and perfecter of our faith…".

Proverbs 21:5 instructs us that, "Steady plodding brings prosperity; hasty speculation brings poverty" (TLB).

Taking action, being proactive, and not giving up are principles for living the life of a successful **and** blessed business person. Nothing will be thrown into our laps. No, business prosperity is not an unconditional providential blessing, and yes, conditions are attached. We are to take action and be proactive.

The abilities and giftings God provides for us as individuals should motivate us to action. Sometimes it takes our persistence in doing the same things faithfully with the heart of a servant. Other times, it is time to try new things, new methods and seek new opportunities. Sometimes it is simply the steady plodding that brings success to your business world.

This verse tells us what to do and what to avoid: "Let us throw off everything that hinders and the sin that so easily entangles, and let us run with perseverance the race marked out for us. Let us fix our eyes on Jesus, the author and perfecter of our faith." Hebrews 12:1, 2

Advancing and growing a business on principle requires hard work, diligence and proactivity. Nothing will be handed to you without these requirements. The Bible says that if a person does not work, he should not eat. Now that's a pretty simple yet direct statement. Does God want to bless your business? Of course, He does. Will His blessing come to us if we are lazy, idle, slothful, passive and unwilling to roll up our sleeves and get to work? No, I don't believe so.

Proverbs 21:25, 26

The sluggard's craving will be the death of him, because his hands refuse to work. All day long he craves for more, but the righteous give without sparing.

Taking action, being proactive, not giving up... all are principled requirements that create and build successful businesses.

1 Thessalonians 4:11

Make it your ambition to lead a quiet life, to mind your own business and to work with your hands, just as we told you, so that your daily life may win the respect of outsiders and so that you will not be dependent on anybody.

Proverbs 22:29

Do you see a man skilled in his work? He will serve before kings; he will not serve before obscure men.

Ecclesiastes 9:10

Whatever your hand finds to do, do it with all your might.

Proverbs 20:4

A sluggard does not plow in season; so at harvest time he looks but finds nothing.

According to the above scriptures, we should approach life and work like the ant. Although the ant has no boss, it still works extremely hard to provide for its needs. A lot of people today could learn a valuable lesson from the ant. Some today have the attitude that if I can get someone else to do the work for me, then why should I exert myself.

Why not let someone else do the work; why not let the government provide for me? Many today have little or no initiative, are not able to put themselves to work, and must always have someone else instruct them and supervise them in order to keep them working. The biblical way is for each person to accept the personal responsibility to be a contributor to society and a person of productivity.

A Productive Business Person

What would be the typical job description of a successful business person?

The successful business person is always in the process of bringing his "vision / purpose" into reality. This process can best be compared to a juggler spinning a series of plates on tall narrow poles. As a new plate is set spinning the juggler must return to those plates he started earlier in order to keep up their momentum. The action becomes furious as more plates are spun, and the danger of one or more falling from its pole increases. Like the juggler, the business person sees the end state of all the plates spinning in perfect timing and sequence as his personal vision. His energies are spent on keeping all the components working toward that common goal.

The successful business person can be described in this manner:

- His/ her chosen career is lonely.

- No one seems to understand their work load; or even can understand.

- There is no typical day or week.

- Requires 24 hour / 7 day availability.

- The path is filled with risk.

- Day is maximized with difficulty.

- Potential failure is always there.

- The capacity for mistakes is widespread.

- He/she is disparaged for failing.

- He/she may be disliked for eventual success.

- The path is always exhausting physically, mentally and emotionally.

- Acceptance of responsibility

- Capacity for hard work

- Desire to achieve

- Drive to complete projects

- Nurturing quality

- Optimism

- Organizational ability

- Orientation to excellence

- Reward orientation

Chapter 15

Following Through

I chose to begin this chapter with a story from the Bible. It centers around a person to whom was given a unenviable and gargantuan task. He had the responsibility of implementing, preparing and following through on an assignment that was not only a mammoth undertaking, but one that would often be the recipient of scornful mocking and repulsive gossip.

Noah Prepared For Critical Follow-Through

The world had become very corrupt and God was tired of it. People were not walking and acting as their Creator wished. He had given them a plan for righteous living and humanity was thumbing their nose at it. God searched the earth for righteous people and found Noah. Noah was called a preacher of righteousness (Hebrews 11:7). He walked by faith. He lived by faith. Noah was a man who found grace in the eyes of the Lord.

Genesis 6:5-9

The LORD saw how great man's wickedness on the earth had become, and that every inclination of the thoughts of his heart was only evil all the time. The LORD was grieved that he had made man on the earth, and his heart was filled with pain. So the LORD said, "I will wipe mankind, whom I have created, from the face of the earth — men and animals, and creatures that move along the ground, and birds of the air — for I am grieved that I have made them." But Noah found favor in the eyes of the LORD. This is the ac-

count of Noah. Noah was a righteous man, blameless among the people of his time, and he walked with God.

Noah was directed by God to prepare an ark. He was to organize it from God's blueprint, to build it up from the ground floor, to follow it through for decades and finally to finish the final construction project. After building it he was to fill it with animals and people. He was tasked with developing a master plan for critical follow-through that not only showed his own creativity, but also aligned his vision with the sovereign plan of God. After completion when God said to get in, he was to follow through with the final phase of God's blueprint.

Here is how Noah provided Critical Follow-Through.

According to God's very specific plan, the ark was to be as follows:

- constructed of gopher wood (Genesis 6:14)
- filled with plenty of separate rooms (Genesis 6:14)
- covered inside and out with pitch (Genesis 6:14)
- have a length of three hundred cubits (Genesis 6:15)
- have a width of fifty cubits
- have a height of thirty cubits
- have a built in window (Genesis 6:16)
- have an inside door (Genesis 6:16)
- have a lower deck
- have a second and third upper deck
- was to house Noah, his wife, his sons, and his son's wives (Genesis 6:18)
- house two of every animal species, male and female (Genesis 6:19, 20)
- have provisions, food for his family and the animals (Genesis 6:21)

Additionally Noah had to follow-through in the following ways:

- continue to work non-stop for some hundred and twenty years
- Noah had to plan his own schedule
- mobilize workers and people to build the boat
- mobilize workers and people to gather the food
- mobilize workers and people to gather the animals
- design the blueprint for all construction according to God's plan
- gather construction workers to train
- assign specific tasks for workers to fulfill
- motivate the construction workers to continue building day after day
- encourage the troops for years

Here is what we can learn about "critical follow-through" from Noah.

- God must be our business partner
- it may take years of hard work and follow-through before the job is done
- we may get discouraged in the process of fulfilling our destiny
- others may ridicule our dreams
- impossible plans can be realized
- God has a plan for us to apprehend and follow-through on
- God is watching from above to see whether or not we follow-through on His plan
- We must have a God-given plan (1 Peter 3:20)
- We have our own planning that we must do
- It takes faith to carry out our plans (Hebrews 11:7)

- We must believe that God will do His part
- We must work very hard and do our part
- Others may not always cooperate
- the effort is worth it all even when serving a few (Noah saved 8)
- we will have to plan for alternatives in our follow-through should obstacles come our way
- our planning and follow-through should be visionary and based upon things not currently seen
- our plans should always be aligned with God's sovereign plans
- God will fulfill His part of the plan, but we must do ours in follow-through
- Noah build the boat, God brought the rain
- good follow-through anticipates the "unseen"
- a good planner begins follow-through with the end in mind

Proverbs 21:5

"The plans of the diligent lead to profit as surely as haste leads to poverty".

In the implementation of your business plans, and following through with those specific plans, surround yourself with those whom have already proven themselves in various areas of your business needs. Other Christian business persons will be more than happy to discuss each detail of your planning and implementation phase. Scripture is very clear about matters of counsel. It is also clear that when we struggle in areas of business, we are to seek help from those who have knowledge and experience.

Proverbs 15:22

Plans fail for lack of counsel, but with many advisers they succeed.

Seeking wisdom and getting help is a personal responsibility, a biblical principle and a practical solution to any business problems. It is your responsibility to get spiritual advice and wisdom about your decisions.

Proverbs 4:5-7

Get wisdom, get understanding; do not forget my words or swerve from them. Do not forsake wisdom, and she will protect you; love her, and she will watch over you. Wisdom is supreme; therefore get wisdom. Though it cost all you have, get understanding.

You can have the best intentions regarding a bright business future, but without input from others, your intentions will fail. What people do you know in your life (a church business friend, a personal friend, your pastor, a CPA, a professional in your line of business) that obviously have their personal and business life in order? Approach them and ask for their advice. People love to share their ideas and strategies with others.

Matthew 7:7, 8

Ask and it will be given to you; seek and you will find; knock and the door will be opened to you. For everyone who asks receives; he who seeks finds; and to him who knocks, the door will be opened.

Humble yourself and learn from those around you. Advancing a successful business works hand in hand with personal advancement. What are you doing to prepare yourself in a way that God can bless?

Planning ahead for an eventual result provides a road map to follow with pre-designated milestones. If you don't have a plan, how will you know when you are successful? Without a predetermined road map, how do you know where you are going? Without a target in your crosshair, how will you know if you are pointed in the right direction? You may have laid out the very best of business plans, but with no follow-through, nothing happens.

Be Alert To Wake Up Calls

In every life there are times when we must sit up, listen up and pay attention. There are events in everyone's life that challenge us to pay attention to the things we are doing, the places we are going, the priorities in our day and in general, the way we are living.

Several times throughout my life I have mourned the death of close friends. I once experienced the loss of a good friend and neighbor. My friend's death was unexpected, untimely, and seemed unreasonable. After a great vacation in a warm, sunny resort, he and his wife returned home to immediate sickness which in a very short time period led to his death.

When we receive wake up calls, it's time for immediate action. If we ignore them, we wind up sleepwalking through life, often times missing out on the really important events that make a difference in eternity. These special "call to attention" events in our lives represent opportunities to make decisions or course corrections. Not unlike the pilot of an air or sea craft, when certain atmospheric conditions push the craft off the charted course, certain immediate corrections must be made.

Course corrections are simply changes in our way of doing things or adjustments to be made in our everyday living. These adjustments represent opportunities for decision-making. They are opportunities to make choices; choice points if you will.

When choice points arise, it's time to rethink the basics. What is my purpose in life? What is important to my family? What is important to my future? Why am I on this mountain? Why am I doing things in this fashion? Although few questions have easy answers, just the opportunity to explore the questions and visit them once again is very beneficial.

As it is in the personal side of life, so it is with any business. Some event may happen in the course of doing your regular business that would cause you to receive a wake up call. Possibly your sales are trending downward. Maybe it is the death of a partner. Maybe a trusted customer went out of business and left you with a large unpaid receivable. Perhaps a trusted key staff person went to work for a competitor. Conceivably you have experienced an unexpected and unrecoverable loss.

Maybe a crucial piece of manufacturing equipment went bad and you have no way of replacing it soon. Perhaps you've experienced a lot of labor unrest. Maybe a trusted employee has accused you falsely. Or it could be that after pouring money into a new business, the lack of return on your investment had drained cash and cash flow has become negative. It may be that your banker turned down your request for the renewal of your credit line. The list of possibilities could go on and on.

What is the business person to do when faced with unexpected crisis? Some questions should immediately come to mind. What is the worst thing that could happen to my business if I address this issue. What is the worst thing that could happen to me or my business if I do not address this issue. Is inaction or action better at this time? If I choose inaction, what could happen to my business?

When faced with forks in our business road, one could react in a negative fashion. Examples: It's not my fault! Why did he/she do this to me? Why does it have to happen in my business? Why did that customer make me the target? It's not fair the my employee did this to me after all I have done for him/her. That vendor has no right to demand cash for my purchases. The nerve of that bank to require monthly financial reports from my business! My name and credit has always been good!

Blaming others does little good. It benefits no one. Whether it is the fault of someone else, ourselves or just the result of market forces, really makes little or no difference at all. What is important is that we take control of the situation, face the music and take some accountability for the future of our business.

If we believe that external forces are responsible for our problems, we have a tendency to do nothing about it. Many a business has been lost because of inaction. On the other hand, if accept accountability for the future of our life, the lives of our family members, our business, and our employed professionals, then it becomes very possible to view our current problems as opportunities for change and adjustment.

What are you learning from this experience? How will your business be affected as the result of your changes? Learning from an unpleasant, unexpected and perhaps uncontrollable experience engages us in new awareness, new insight, new diligence and the ability to turn the present situation around. When it comes to unpleasant circumstances the way out is often through.

Summary

Business success can be made or broken by the habits you form. Our habits have great influence upon our success in life. Habits can be major obstacles to becoming successful. Habits can be the foundation of your successes. Every person who is successful has simply formed the habits of doing things that failures dislike doing and will not do.

Business success is also about finding the barriers to developing and implementing new ideas and removing them. The only way to get something you want is to put in the effort required to get it. There are no easy answers, no get-rich-quick schemes, just plenty of scams which will only serve to derail you from your potential success.

Without a vision, without purpose, no goals can be met. A lack of goals leads to a lack of planning and inaction. Know your purpose for being in business. Make wise decisions. Don't let emotion lead you astray or let a fear of being wrong hold you back from making decisions.

To achieve quality, you must ask for it, expect it, require it, and reward it. Excellence breeds excellence. Without quality, you will not have any customers, and without customers, you will not have a business.

There is much value in learning to ask for help and support, and finding the resources for getting the help you need. Whether you're eager to begin your business or simply reach your next goal, accept that "your turn will come." However this doesn't mean settling for inaction. Being patient isn't the same as being complacent.

Follow-through is vital to the success of all businesses. No goals are every reached without great follow-through. To do so takes great discipline. Personal discipline is a key to success.

Persistence is perhaps the most essential quality needed to attain success both in your professional career and in your personal life. If you throw in the towel every time you face adversity, you'll never know how a winner feels. When the going gets rough, stay in the ring and slug it out.

Successful people are truly creative. They envision alternatives. They are curious, always trying out new possibilities. The entrepreneur achieves success through innovation.

My hat is off to you. Go, Grow & Advance. Be Successful!

I know you can do it!

Bibliography

A special thanks goes out to those sources whom I do not know and have not been successful in documenting. Over the years I have collected bits and pieces of interesting material—written notes on sermons and lectures I've heard, jotted-down comments on financial articles I've read, and a lot of other great information.

Because I have written parts of this text over a period of many years and have not always been able to completely document exactly every source of information, this bibliography may not be entirely complete. While I would prefer to list the source reference of every thought and idea covered, I simply cannot.

The following list is in alphabetical order and will serve to give you sources for much of what you find in this book. I extend my appreciation to the many sermons, articles, and/or books from authors, teachers, etc., from which I have taken notes but, in the early years, failed to record the source.

Rich Brott

Book Resources

Abrams, Rhonda. *The Successful Business Plan*. Rhonda Incorporated, 2003.

Anders, Max. *21 Unbreakable Laws of Life*. Thomas Nelson, 1996.

Bach, David. *The Automatic Millionaire*. Broadway, 2003.

———. T*he Finish Rich Workbook, workbook edition*. Broadway, 2003.

Bain, Dwight. *Destination Success*. Baker Publishing Group, 2003.

Baker, Roland, and Heidi. *Always Enough*. Baker Publishing Group, 2003.

Blue, Ron. *Splitting Heirs*. Moody Press, 2004.

———. *Storm Shelter*. Thomas Nelson Incorporated, 1994.

———. *Taming the Money Monster: 5 Steps to Conquering Debt*. Tyndale House Publishers, 2000.

Briner, Bob. *Business Basics from the Bible—More Ancient Wisdom for Modern Business*. Zondervan, 1996.

———. *The Management Methods of Jesus*. Thomas Nelson, 1996.

Brott, Rich. Biblical Principles for Becoming Debt Free. City Bible Publishing, 2005.

———. *Biblical Principles for Releasing Financial Provision*. City Bible Publishing, 2005.

———. *Family Finance Handbook*. City Bible Publishing, 2004.

Burkett, Larry, and Ron Blue. *Wealth to Last*. Broadman & Holman Publishers, 2003.

Burkett, Larry. *Business By the Book*. Thomas Nelson, 1998.

Burton, E. James. *Total Business Planning*. Wiley, 1999.

Barnes, W. G. *Business in the Bible—1925*. Kessinger Publishing, 2003.

Chewning, Richard. *Biblical Principles and Business: The Practice*. Navpress, 1989.

Clements, Patrick. *Financial Freedom*. VMI Publishers, 2003.

Collins, Susan Ford. *The Joy of Success*. Quill, 2004.

Colson, Charles B. *Eight Steps to Seven Figures*. Double Day, 2000.

Cook, Wade. *Business Buy the Bible*. Lighthouse Publishing Incorporated, 1997.

Cummuta, John. *Are You Being Seduced into Debt?* Thomas Nelson, 2004.

Damazio, Frank. *Effective Keys to Successful Leadership*. City Bible Publishing, 1993.

———. *The Making of a Leader*. City Bible Publishing, 1988.

———. *The Making of a Vision*. City Bible Publishing, 2002.

———. *Vanguard Leader*. City Bible Publishing, 1994.

Dayton, Edward. *Succeeding in Business Without Losing Your Faith*. Baker Publishing Group, 1992.

Duncan, Todd. *The Power to Be Your Best*. Thomas Nelson, 2004.

Duncan, Todd. *High Trust Selling*. Thomas Nelson, 2002.

Fehrenbacher, Scott. *Put Your Money Where Your Morals Are*. Broadman & Holman Publishers, 2001.

Floyd, Mike. *Supernatural Business*. Creation House, 2003.

Goldstein, Dr. Arnold. *The Business Doctor*. Garrett Publishing Incorporated, 1994.

Grudem, Wayne. *Business for the Glory of God: The Bible's Teaching on the Moral Goodness of Business*. Crossway Books, 2003.

Hagin, Kenneth. *Biblical Keys to Financial Prosperity*. Faith Library Publications, 1995.

Hammond, Bob. *Life Without Debt: Free Yourself from the Burden of Money Worries*. Career Press Incorporated, 1995.

Hancock, Wayne. *Understanding Biblical Prosperity*. Xulon Press, 2003.

Hirsch, Peter. *Success by Design*. Bethany House, 2002.

Hybels, Bill, Charles Swindoll, and Larry Burkett. *The Life@Work Book*. Word Books, 2000.

Johnson, Spencer. *Who Moved My Cheese?* Putnam Publishing Group, 2000.

Jones, Laurie Beth. *Jesus CEO*. Hyperion, 1995.

Julian, Larry. *God Is My CEO*. Adams Media Corporation, 2001.

Katz, Robert. *Biblical Roads to Financial Freedom*. Destiny Image, 2003.

Kise, Jane. *Working with Purpose*. Augsgurg Fortress, 2004.

Leman, Kevin. *Winning the Rat Race Without Becoming a Rat*. Thomas Nelson, 1996.

Livingstone, John, and Theodore Grossman. *The Portable MBA in Finance and Accounting*. John Wiley & Sons Incorporated, 2001.

Loyker, Herbert. *All the Trades and Occupations of the Bible*. Zodervan, 1988.

Luce, Donald. *Time-Out Leadership*. Thomas Nelson, 1995.

MacAdam, Millard. *Intentional Integrity*. Broadman & Holman Publishers, 1996.

Malphurs, Aubrey. *Values-Driven Leadership*. Baker Publishing Group, 2004.

Marr, Steve. *Business Proverbs*. Fleming H. Revell, 2001.

Marshall, Rich, and Tommy Tenney. *God at Work: Discovering the Anointing for Business*. Destiny Image Publishers, 2000.

Mason, John. *The Impossible Is Possible*. Bethany House Publishers, 2003.

Maxwell, John. *Thinking for a Change*. Warner Books, 2003.

———. *Your Road Map for Success*. Thomas Nelson, 2003.

McCarthy. *The On-Purpose Business: Doing More of What You Do Best More Profitably*. Pinon Press, 2002.

Miller, Calvin. *The Empowered Leader.* Broadman & Holman Publishers, 1995.

Munroe, Myles. *The Principles and Power of Vision.* Whitaker House, 2003.

Myers, Wayne. *Living Beyond the Possible.* Evangeline Press, 2003.

Novak, Michael. *Business As a Calling.* Simon & Schuster Incorporated, 1996.

Ostrom, Don. *Millionaire in the Pew: Keys to Faith for Prosperity and Freedom from Poverty.* Insight Publishing Group, 2004.

Palmen, Ralph. *8 Critical Lifetime Decisions.* Beacon Hill Press, 2002.

Patsula, Peter. *Successful Business Planning in 30 Days.* Patsula Media, 2004.

Pollan, Stephan M., and Mark Levine. *Die Broke.* HarperBusiness, 1997.

Robinson, David. *What Is an Entrepreneur?* Adams Media Corporation, 1992.

Silvoso, Ed. *Anointed for Business.* Regal, 2002.

Stanley, Thomas. *The Millionaire Mind.* Andrews McMeel Publishing, 2001.

———. *The Millionaire Next Door.* Pocket Books, 1998.

Steward, David L. *Doing Business by the Good Book.* Hyperion Press, 2004.

Taylor, Don. *Solid Gold Success Strategies for Your Business.* AMACOM, 1996.

Magazine Resources

Business Week

Forbes

Fortune Magazine

Smart Money

US News and World Report

Newspaper Resources

Barrons

Wall Street Journal

Washington Times

Online Resources

BusinessWeek (http://www.businessweek.com)

Forbes (www.forbes.com)

Fortune Magazine (http://www.fortune.com)

National Federation of Independent Business (http://www.nfib.com)

United States Federation of Small Businesses (http://www.usfsb.com)

Additional Resources *by Rich Brott*

www.RichBrott.com

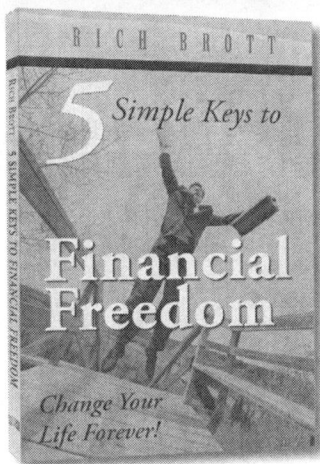

5 Simple Keys to Financial Freedom

Change Your Life Forever!

By Rich Brott

6" x 9", 108 pages
ISBN 1-60185-022-0
ISBN (EAN) 978-1-60185-022-5

abc
Book Publishing

Order online at:
www.RichBrott.com
www.amazon.com
www.barnesandnoble.com
www.booksamillion.com
www.citychristianpublishing.com
www.bordersstores.com

www.AbcBookPublishing.com

Additional Resources *by Rich Brott*

www.RichBrott.com

10 Life-Changing Attitudes That Will Make You a Financial Success

By Rich Brott

6" x 9", 108 pages
ISBN 1-60185-021-2
ISBN (EAN) 978-1-60185-021-8

a b c

Book Publishing

Order online at:

www.RichBrott.com
www.amazon.com
www.barnesandnoble.com
www.booksamillion.com
www.citychristianpublishing.com
www.bordersstores.com

www.AbcBookPublishing.com

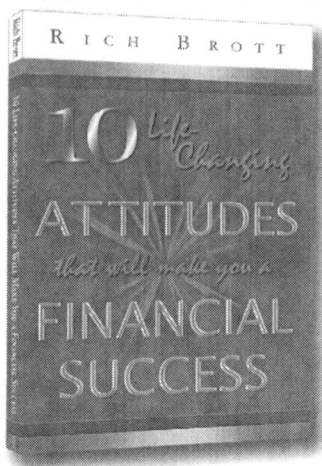

Additional Resources *by Rich Brott*

www.RichBrott.com

R I C H   B R O T T

15 Biblical Responsibilities

leading to

Financial Wisdom

Accepting personal accountability

15 Biblical Responsibilities
Leading to Financial Wisdom

Accepting Personal Accountability

By Rich Brott

6" x 9", 120 pages
ISBN 1-60185-010-7
ISBN (EAN) 978-1-60185-010-2

Order online at:
www.RichBrott.com
www.amazon.com
www.barnesandnoble.com
www.booksamillion.com
www.citychristianpublishing.com
www.bordersstores.com

abc
Book Publishing

www.AbcBookPublishing.com

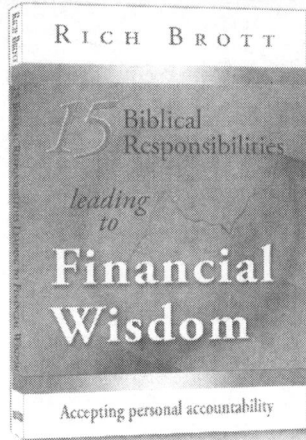

Additional Resources *by Rich Brott*

www.RichBrott.com

30 Biblical Principles for Managing Your Money

Insights that Will Set You Free!

By Rich Brott

6" x 9", 160 pages
ISBN 1-60185-012-3
ISBN (EAN) 978-1-60185-012-6

abc
Book Publishing

Order online at:
www.RichBrott.com
www.amazon.com
www.barnesandnoble.com
www.booksamillion.com
www.citychristianpublishing.com
www.bordersstores.com

www.AbcBookPublishing.com

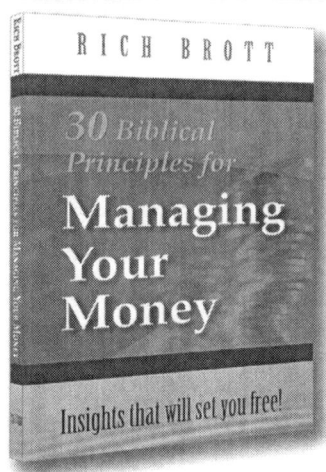

Additional Resources *by Rich Brott*

www.RichBrott.com

35 Keys to
Financial Independence

Finding the Freedom You Seek!

By Rich Brott

6" x 9", 176 pages
ISBN 1-60185-020-4
ISBN (EAN) 978-1-60185-020-1

a b c
Book Publishing

Order online at:

www.RichBrott.com
www.amazon.com
www.barnesandnoble.com
www.booksamillion.com
www.citychristianpublishing.com
www.bordersstores.com

www.AbcBookPublishing.com

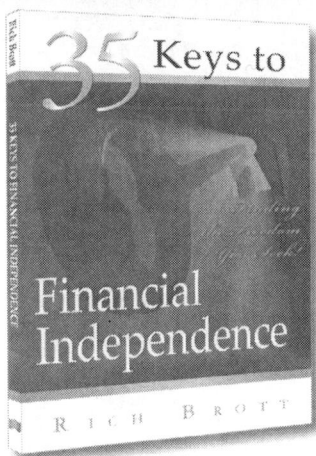

Additional Resources *by Rich Brott*

www.RichBrott.com

A Biblical Perspective on
Giving Generously
Learning How to Receive God's Blessings

By Rich Brott
6" x 9" - 172 pages
ISBN 1-60185-000-X
ISBN (EAN) 978-1-60185-000-3

abc
Book Publishing

Order online at:
www.RichBrott.com
www.amazon.com
www.barnesandnoble.com
www.booksamillion.com
www.citychristianpublishing.com
www.bordersstores.com

www.AbcBookPublishing.com

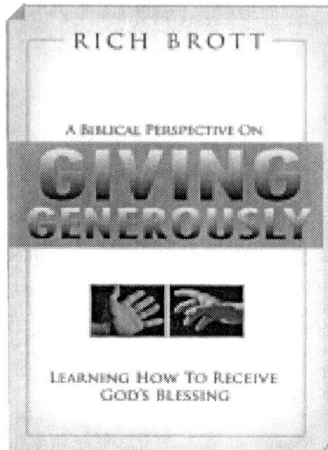

Additional Resources *by Rich Brott*

www.RichBrott.com

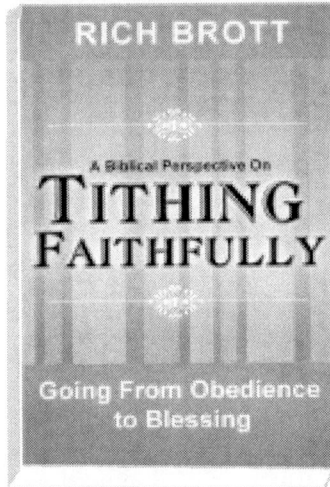

A Biblical Perspective on
Tithing Faithfully
Going From Obedience to Blessings

By Rich Brott
6" x 9" - 148 pages
ISBN 1-60185-001-8
ISBN (EAN) 978-1-60185-001-0

a b c
Book Publishing

Order online at:
www.RichBrott.com
www.amazon.com
www.barnesandnoble.com
www.booksamillion.com
www.citychristianpublishing.com
www.bordersstores.com

www.AbcBookPublishing.com

Additional Resources *by Rich Brott*

www.RichBrott.com

RICH BROTT

ACHIEVING FINANCIAL ALIGNMENT

30 Biblical Principles
for Ordering Your Financial Life

Achieving Financial Alignment

30 Biblical Principles for Ordering Your Financial Life

By Rich Brott

6" x 9", 148 pages
ISBN 1-60185-011-5
ISBN (EAN) 978-1-60185-011-9

a|b|c
Book Publishing

Order online at:
www.RichBrott.com
www.amazon.com
www.barnesandnoble.com
www.booksamillion.com
www.citychristianpublishing.com
www.bordersstores.com

www.AbcBookPublishing.com

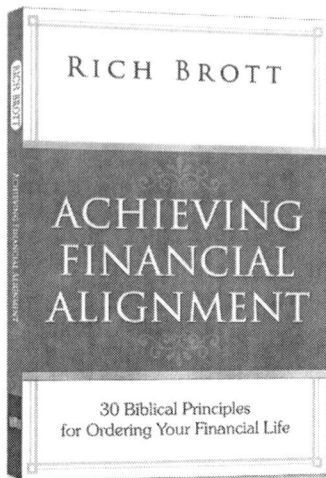

Additional Resources *by Rich Brott*

www.RichBrott.com

RICH BROTT

ACTIVATING
Your Personal
FAITH
To RECEIVE

25 Biblical Principles for
Releasing the Power Within!

Activating Your Personal Faith To Receive

25 Biblical Principles for Releasing the Power Within!

By Rich Brott

6" x 9", 148 pages
ISBN 1-60185-008-5
ISBN (EAN) 978-1-60185-008-9

abc
Book Publishing

Order online at:
www.RichBrott.com
www.amazon.com
www.barnesandnoble.com
www.booksamillion.com
www.citychristianpublishing.com
www.bordersstores.com

www.AbcBookPublishing.com

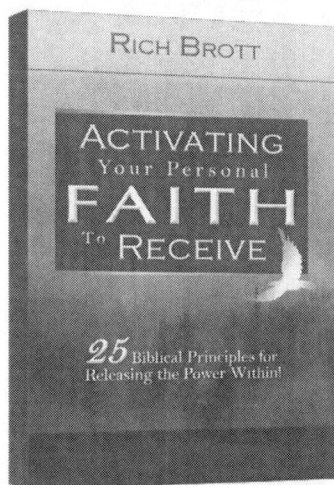

Additional Resources *by Rich Brott*

www.RichBrott.com

RICH BROTT

ALL THE
FINANCIAL
SCRIPTURES
IN THE BIBLE

WITH
COMMENTARY

All the Financial Scriptures in the Bible with Commentary

By Rich Brott

6" x 9", 364 pages
ISBN 1-60185-004-2
ISBN (EAN) 978-1-60185-004-1

a b c

Book Publishing

Order online at:

www.RichBrott.com
www.amazon.com
www.barnesandnoble.com
www.booksamillion.com
www.citychristianpublishing.com
www.bordersstores.com

www.AbcBookPublishing.com

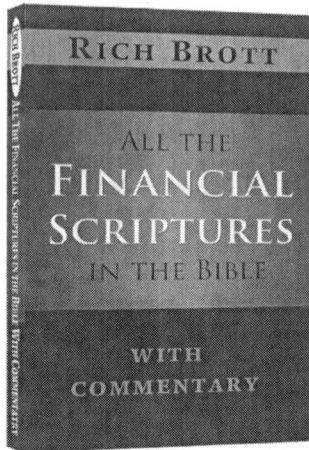

Additional Resources *by Rich Brott*

www.RichBrott.com

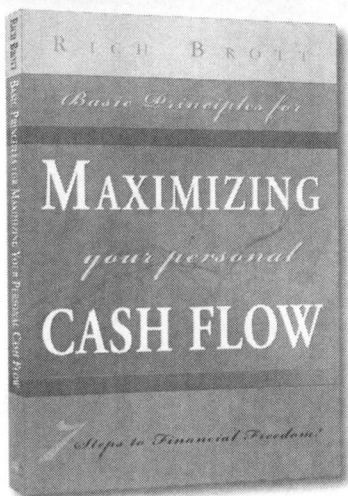

Basic Principles for Maximizing Your Personal Cash Flow

7 Steps to Financial Freedom!

By Rich Brott

6" x 9", 120 pages
ISBN 1-60185-019-0
ISBN (EAN) 978-1-60185-019-5

abc
Book Publishing

Order online at:
www.RichBrott.com
www.amazon.com
www.barnesandnoble.com
www.booksamillion.com
www.citychristianpublishing.com
www.bordersstores.com

www.AbcBookPublishing.com

Additional Resources *by Rich Brott*

www.RichBrott.com

Basic Principles of Conservative Investing

9 Principles You Must Follow

By Rich Brott

6" x 9", 116 pages
ISBN 1-60185-018-2
ISBN (EAN) 978-1-60185-018-8

abc
Book Publishing

Order online at:
www.RichBrott.com
www.amazon.com
www.barnesandnoble.com
www.booksamillion.com
www.citychristianpublishing.com
www.bordersstores.com

www.AbcBookPublishing.com

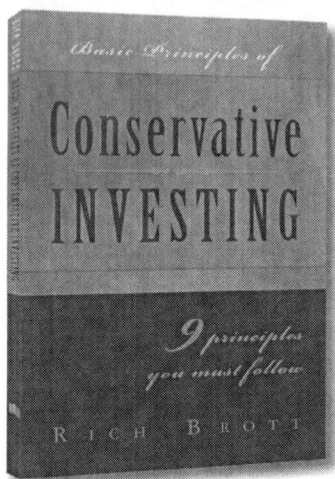

Additional Resources *by Rich Brott*

www.RichBrott.com

RICH BROTT

BIBLICAL PRINCIPLES FOR

ACHIEVING PERSONAL SUCCESS

8 CRITICAL INSIGHTS YOU MUST DISCOVER!

Biblical Principles for Achieving Personal Success

8 Critical Insights You Must Discover!

By Rich Brott

6" x 9", 248 pages
ISBN 1-60185-013-1
ISBN (EAN) 978-1-60185-013-3

abc
Book Publishing

Order online at:

www.RichBrott.com
www.amazon.com
www.barnesandnoble.com
www.booksamillion.com
www.citychristianpublishing.com
www.bordersstores.com

www.AbcBookPublishing.com

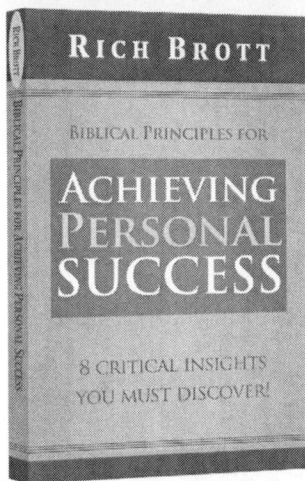

Additional Resources *by Rich Brott*

www.RichBrott.com

Biblical Principles for Staying Out of Debt

7 Things You Must Know!

By Rich Brott

6" x 9", 120 pages
ISBN 1-60185-009-3
ISBN (EAN) 978-1-60185-009-6

abc
Book Publishing

Order online at:

www.RichBrott.com
www.amazon.com
www.barnesandnoble.com
www.booksamillion.com
www.citychristianpublishing.com
www.bordersstores.com

www.AbcBookPublishing.com

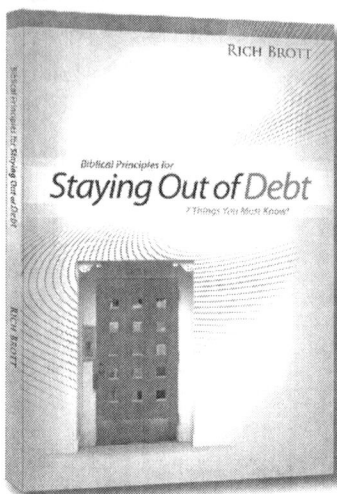

Additional Resources *by Rich Brott*

www.RichBrott.com

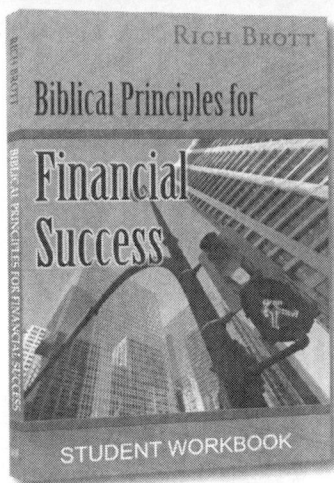

Biblical Principles for Financial Success

Student Workbook

By Rich Brott

7.5" x 9.25", 228 pages
ISBN 1-60185-016-6
ISBN (EAN) 978-1-60185-016-4

abc
Book Publishing

Order online at:
www.RichBrott.com
www.amazon.com
www.barnesandnoble.com
www.booksamillion.com
www.citychristianpublishing.com
www.bordersstores.com

www.AbcBookPublishing.com

Additional Resources *by Rich Brott*

www.RichBrott.com

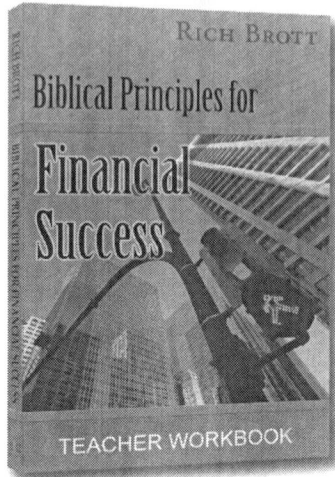

Biblical Principles for Financial Success

Teacher Workbook

By Rich Brott

7.5" x 9.25", 228 pages
ISBN 1-60185-015-8
ISBN (EAN) 978-1-60185-015-7

a|b|c
Book Publishing

Order online at:

www.RichBrott.com
www.amazon.com
www.barnesandnoble.com
www.booksamillion.com
www.citychristianpublishing.com
www.bordersstores.com

www.AbcBookPublishing.com

Additional Resources *by Rich Brott*

www.RichBrott.com

Biblical Principles that Create Success through Productivity

How God Blesses Our Work Ethic

By Rich Brott

6" x 9", 224 pages
ISBN 1-60185-007-7
ISBN (EAN) 978-1-60185-007-2

a b c
Book Publishing

Order online at:

www.RichBrott.com
www.amazon.com
www.barnesandnoble.com
www.booksamillion.com
www.citychristianpublishing.com
www.bordersstores.com

www.AbcBookPublishing.com

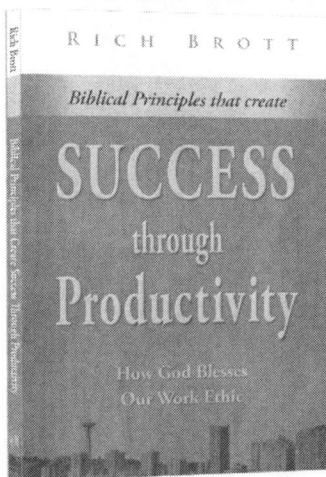

Additional Resources *by Rich Brott*

www.RichBrott.com

Business, Occupations, Professions & Vocations in the Bible

By Rich Brott

6" x 9", 212 pages
ISBN 1-60185-014-X
ISBN (EAN) 978-1-60185-014-0

abc
Book Publishing

Order online at:
www.RichBrott.com
www.amazon.com
www.barnesandnoble.com
www.booksamillion.com
www.citychristianpublishing.com
www.bordersstores.com

www.AbcBookPublishing.com

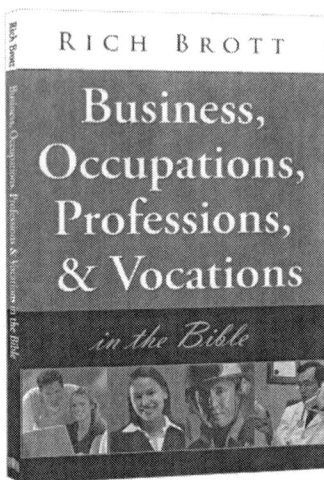

Additional Resources *by Rich Brott*

www.RichBrott.com

How to Receive
Prosperity & Provision

17 Principles You Must Know

By Rich Brott

6" x 9", 296 pages
ISBN 1-60185-005-0
ISBN (EAN) 978-1-60185-005-8

a b c
Book Publishing

Order online at:
www.RichBrott.com
www.amazon.com
www.barnesandnoble.com
www.booksamillion.com
www.citychristianpublishing.com
www.bordersstores.com

www.AbcBookPublishing.com

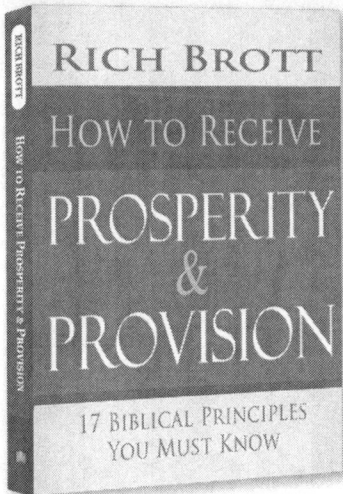

www.RichBrott.com

Prosperity Has a Purpose!

27 Biblical Principles to Understand

By Rich Brott

6" x 9", 276 pages
ISBN 1-60185-006-9
ISBN (EAN) 978-1-60185-006-5

abc
Book Publishing

Order online at:
www.RichBrott.com
www.amazon.com
www.barnesandnoble.com
www.booksamillion.com
www.citychristianpublishing.com
www.bordersstores.com

www.AbcBookPublishing.com

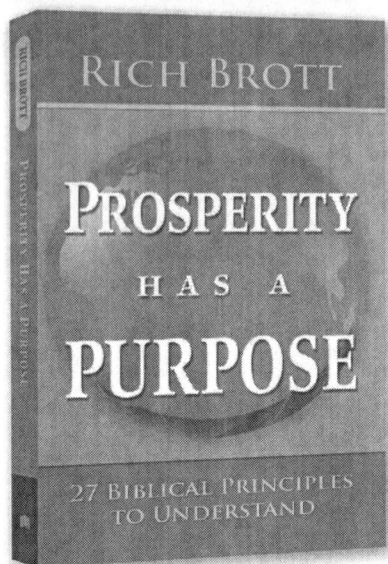

Additional Resources *by Rich Brott*

www.RichBrott.com

RICH BROTT

SUCCESSFUL
TIME
MANAGEMENT

Be the Productive Person
You Want to Be!

Successful Time Management

Be the Productive Person You Want to Be!

By Rich Brott

6" x 9", 104 pages
ISBN 1-60185-017-4
ISBN (EAN) 978-1-60185-017-1

a b c
Book Publishing

Order online at:
www.RichBrott.com
www.amazon.com
www.barnesandnoble.com
www.booksamillion.com
www.citychristianpublishing.com
www.bordersstores.com

www.AbcBookPublishing.com

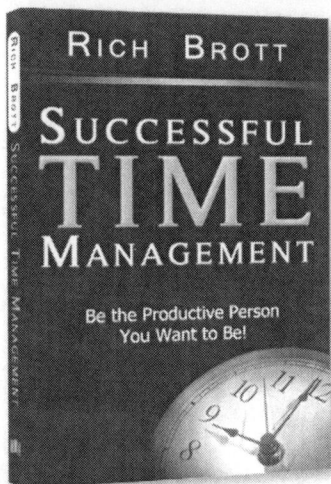

Additional Resources *by Rich Brott*

www.RichBrott.com

Biblical Principles for Success in Personal Finance

Your Roadmap to Financial Independence

By Rich Brott

7.5" x 10", 519 pages
ISBN 0-914936-72-7
ISBN (EAN) 978-0-914936-72-5

a|b|c
Book Publishing

Order online at:
www.RichBrott.com
www.amazon.com
www.barnesandnoble.com
www.booksamillion.com
www.citychristianpublishing.com
www.bordersstores.com

www.AbcBookPublishing.com

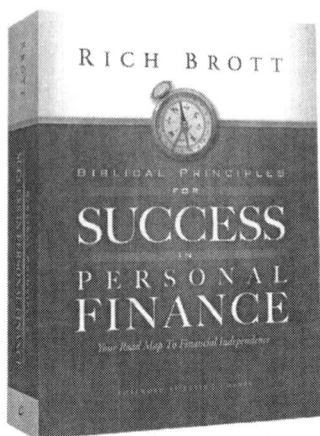

Additional Resources *by Rich Brott*

www.RichBrott.com

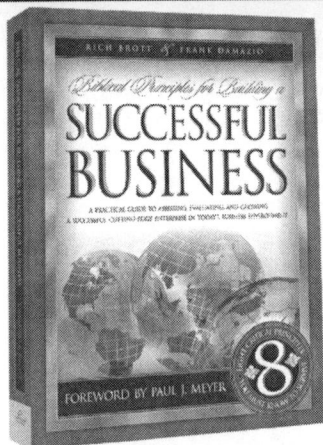

Biblical Principles for Building a Successful Business

A Practical Guide to Assessing, Evaluating, and Growing a Successful Cutting-Edge Enterprise in Today's Business Environment

By Rich Brott & Frank Damazio

7.5" x 10", 477 pages
ISBN 1-59383-027-0
ISBN (EAN) 978-1-59383-027-4

abc
Book Publishing

Order online at:
www.RichBrott.com
www.amazon.com
www.barnesandnoble.com
www.booksamillion.com
www.citychristianpublishing.com
www.bordersstores.com

www.AbcBookPublishing.com

Additional Resources *by Rich Brott*

www.RichBrott.com

RICH BROTT · FRANK DAMAZIO

Biblical Principles
for becoming
Debt Free!

RESCUE YOUR LIFE & LIBERATE YOUR FUTURE

5 Keys | 10 Attitudes | 15 Responsibilities
30 Biblical Principles | 35 Practical Applications

Biblical Principles for
Becoming Debt Free!

*Rescue Your Life and
Liberate Your Future!*

By Rich Brott & Frank Damazio

7.5" x 10", 320 pages
ISBN 1-886849-85-4
ISBN 978-1-886849-85-3

abc
Book Publishing

Order online at:
www.RichBrott.com
www.amazon.com
www.barnesandnoble.com
www.booksamillion.com
www.citychristianpublishing.com
www.bordersstores.com

www.AbcBookPublishing.com

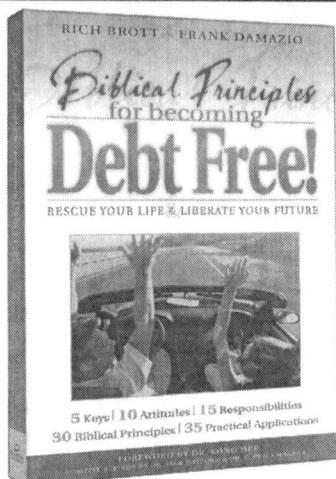

Additional Resources *by Rich Brott*

www.RichBrott.com

Biblical Principles for Releasing Financial Provision!

Obtaining the Favor of God in Your
Personal and Business World

By Rich Brott

7.5" x 10", 456 pages
ISBN 1-59383-021-1
ISBN (EAN) 978-1-59383-021-2

abc
Book Publishing

Order online at:
www.RichBrott.com
www.amazon.com
www.barnesandnoble.com
www.booksamillion.com
www.citychristianpublishing.com
www.bordersstores.com

www.AbcBookPublishing.com

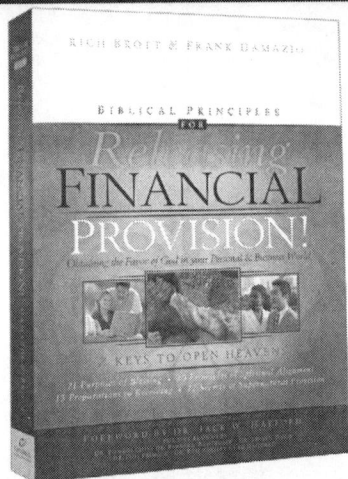

Additional Resources *by Rich Brott*

www.RichBrott.com

RICH BROTT & FRANK DAMAZIO

FAMILY FINANCE HANDBOOK

DISCOVERING THE BLESSINGS OF FINANCIAL FREEDOM

FOREWORD BY DR. DAVID YONGGI CHO

Family Finance Handbook

Discovering the Blessing
of Financial Freedom

By Rich Brott & Frank Damazio

7.5" x 10", 288 pages
ISBN 1-914936-60-3
ISBN 978-1-914936-60-2

abc
Book Publishing

Order online at:
www.RichBrott.com
www.amazon.com
www.barnesandnoble.com
www.booksamillion.com
www.citychristianpublishing.com
www.bordersstores.com

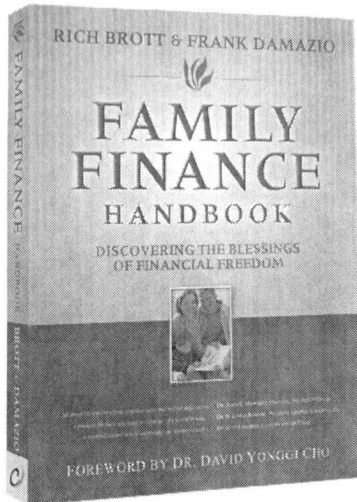

Additional Resources *by Rich Brott*

www.RichBrott.com

A Biblical Perspective on Tithing & Giving

A Believer's Stewardship Guide

By Rich Brott

6" x 9", 172 pages
ISBN 1-60185-000-X
ISBN (EAN) 978-1-60185-000-3

a b c
Book Publishing

Order online at:
www.RichBrott.com
www.amazon.com
www.barnesandnoble.com
www.booksamillion.com
www.citychristianpublishing.com
www.bordersstores.com

www.AbcBookPublishing.com

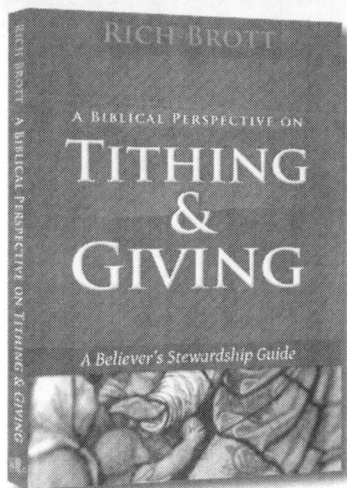

Additional Resources *by Rich Brott*

www.RichBrott.com

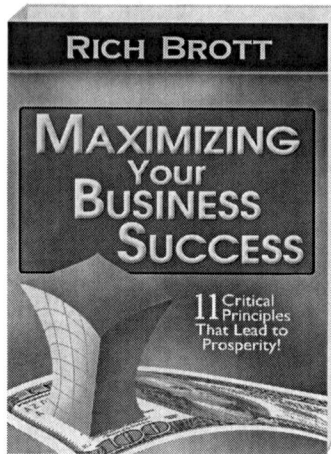

Maximizing Your Business Success
11 Critical Principles That Lead to Prosperity!

By Rich Brott
6" x 9" - 319 pages
ISBN 1-60185-023-9
ISBN (EAN) 978-1-60185-023-2

a b c
Book Publishing

Order online at:
www.RichBrott.com
www.amazon.com
www.barnesandnoble.com
www.booksamillion.com
www.citychristianpublishing.com
www.bordersstores.com

www.AbcBookPublishing.com

Additional Resources *by Rich Brott*

www.RichBrott.com

Establishing a Successful Business
Fast-track Your Opportunities!

By Rich Brott
6" x 9" - 273 pages
ISBN: 1-60185-024-7
ISBN (EAN): 978-1-60185-024-9

abc
Book Publishing

Order online at:
www.RichBrott.com
www.amazon.com
www.barnesandnoble.com
www.booksamillion.com
www.citychristianpublishing.com
www.bordersstores.com

www.AbcBookPublishing.com

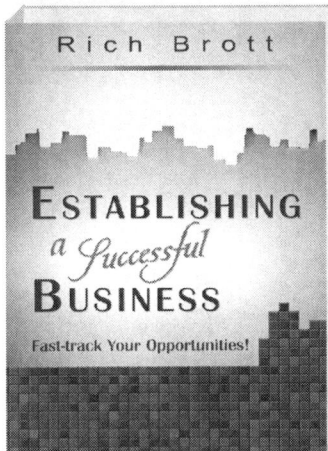

Additional Resources *by Rich Brott*

www.RichBrott.com

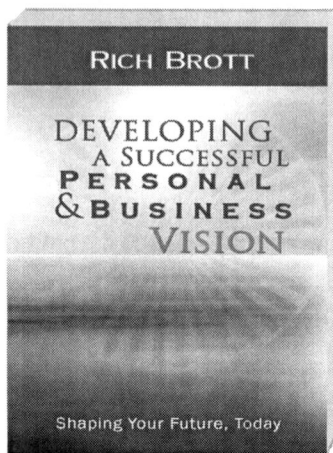

Developing a Successful Personal & Business Vision

Shaping Your Future, Today

By Rich Brott

6" x 9" - 272 pages
ISBN: 1-60185-003-4
ISBN (EAN): 978-1-60185-003-4

a b c
Book Publishing

Order online at:
www.RichBrott.com
www.amazon.com
www.barnesandnoble.com
www.booksamillion.com
www.citychristianpublishing.com
www.bordersstores.com

www.AbcBookPublishing.com

Additional Resources *by Rich Brott*

www.RichBrott.com

Advancing a Successful Business
Managing Your Organization Well!

By Rich Brott
6" x 9" - 243 pages
ISBN: 1-60185-025-5
ISBN (EAN): 978-1-60185-025-6

abc
Book Publishing

Order online at:
www.RichBrott.com
www.amazon.com
www.barnesandnoble.com
www.booksamillion.com
www.citychristianpublishing.com
www.bordersstores.com

www.AbcBookPublishing.com

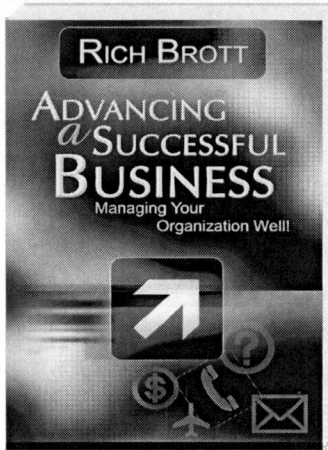

Printed in the United States
202155BV00003B/1-120/P

9 781601 850256